SPEAKING FROM *The Shadows*

A PASTOR'S RESPONSE TO EMOTIONAL DARKNESS

"Even though I walk through the valley of the shadow of death, I will fear no evil, for you are with me; your rod and your staff, they comfort me."

Psalm 23:4 ESV

WESTBOW
PRESS®
A DIVISION OF THOMAS NELSON
& ZONDERVAN

WestBow Press books may be ordered through booksellers or by contacting:

WestBow Press
A Division of Thomas Nelson & Zondervan
1663 Liberty Drive
Bloomington, IN 47403
www.westbowpress.com
844-714-3454

ISBN: 979-8-3850-0398-3 (sc)
ISBN: 979-8-3850-0399-0 (hc)
ISBN: 979-8-3850-0400-3 (e)

Library of Congress Control Number: 2023914128

Print information available on the last page.

WestBow Press rev. date: 07/31/2023

Cover and Layout Design: Camryn Fazal
Author's Photo: Noelle Photography
Lantern Logo Design: Molly Kate Jubril

"'With much knowledge comes much sorrow.' That's in the Bible. And it's true. The more we learn about ourselves, about others, and about the world we live in, the more prone we are to feel hopeless and overwhelmed. Today we know more in all these areas than ever before. I suspect our increased knowledge has indeed amplified our sorrow in proportion.

In the dark, we want to know we're not alone, we're somewhere on the normal spectrum, and we'll make it.

This is where my long-time friend, David Barringer, comes in. Dave is a person of spiritual integrity, a faithful pastor, and a good husband and father. His experience with depression reminds us that it doesn't strike bad people or unspiritual people. It will take anybody.

I am sure it has been painful to him, but I am grateful he has shared his story with the rest of us. I am confident reading his experience will answer many people's heart cry to know they are not alone, that they are somewhere on the normal spectrum, and that they will make it through."

— *J.P. Dorsey*
Former President of Northpoint Bible College - Grand Rapids, MI

"More than anyone I know, Dave Barringer can make others feel seen and heard by sharing his experiences. Operating with a high level of emotional intelligence, Dave corrects, challenges, and inspires people to pursue wholeness. If you need help dealing with your darkness, this book will help you find freedom."

— *Peter Reeves | Founder of Reeves Initiative*

"I have had the privilege of knowing Dave for years. He and I have had many conversations about this topic. I very much appreciate the way that he shares his heart and always steers people back to God. There are so many people that will be helped by this book"

— *Barry Brigham, MA, LPC, LLP*
Founder and President of Cornerstone Counseling Center

"Many pastors feel they cannot be forthcoming regarding their own struggles with mental health and depression for fear of negative ministerial ramifications. Dave is tackling a difficult, yet vital, task as he tells his story and offers insight. This book is a "must" on anyone's bookshelf."

— *Aaron Hlavin*
Superintendent of the Michigan Ministry Network, Assemblies of God

"A powerful, personal, and honest journey into the shadows of depression merging the reality of pain with the path to hope and healing. This book sheds a light on the darkest experiences never said out loud and the practical help needed to a brighter future."

— *Curt Demoff | Lead Pastor of Bridgewood Church*

"Dave Barringer's deep reservoir of spiritual, professional, and personal abilities profoundly benefit his family, friends, congregants, and readers. His latest literary work, "Speaking from the Shadows" skillfully sheds light on "dark forces of depression" that can lead to trauma, feelings of inadequacy, hopelessness, and isolation. His authenticity as he transparently unpacks his personal journey with depression is refreshing. He provides his readers with reasons to hope, helps them conceptualize and communicate about depression, and encourages them to focus on the future as they embrace their value. As Pastor Dave points out, depression can hit anyone. Chances are you either know someone battling with depression or you may battle with it yourself. I highly recommend this read to all who are interested in the topic of depression."

— Cindy Grimmer, OTR, MA, LPC
President and Founder of Kalamazoo Christian Counseling

"Dave Barringer is one of the most authentic voices on a myriad of topics; when I found out he was doing a book on mental health I couldn't contain my excitement. Dave speaks from a place of honest experience and remarkable expertise to help anyone gain a better perspective on their perspectives. Speaking from the Shadows is a must for anyone who wants to better themselves and the people around them."

— Ty Buckingham | Author and Speaker

"David Barringer is a leading voice on the subject of depression. David's transparency about his struggle with the "long dark tunnel" has inspired many leaders to open up about their own challenges with depression. In this book David taps into his own experience and outlines a practical pathway toward health."

— John Opalewski | Founder of Converge Coaching

"Pastor Dave's willingness to use his own story and heart as a pastor to normalize discussions surrounding mental health has already helped so many feel seen, understood and hopeful. This book is an extension of the gift God has given him to give language to what so many people struggle with and don't quite have the words to articulate. Whether you struggle with mental health yourself or simply want to know how to be a friend to those that do, this book is for you."

— Chris Davis | Pastor and Director of Potomac School of Leadership

I dedicate this book to a friend who passed away a few years ago. He's the one who helped encourage me to put words to my depression and to take action to get healthier.

Jarrid, I miss our Twitter interactions and our texts during MMA fights. I miss seeing your face and your posts pop up on social media.

You were an anthem of hope to many.
Your life is still an inspiration to others.

Love and appreciate you my friend.

To my friend Julia
Thanks for your encouragement to continue to write.
Thanks for your push to get this project done.
Thanks for the investment of your time to help me shape my writing voice.

Thanks for the debates over phrases and wordings.
Most of all, thanks for believing in the potential of what this book can be for the lives of people hurting in the shadows.
I couldn't have completed this book without you.

For every person who finds themselves in the shadows,
For every human who journeys through the darkest valley,
For every soul that has been fractured by what lives in the night:

We have a Light.
We have a Hope.
His name is Jesus.

CONTENTS

PROLOGUE

I'm a pastor who deals with depression. I tend to refer to it as the "shadows." Personally, I've had to navigate them most of my life.

I bring up my title not to build up a pedestal, label, or an achievement I've attained, but rather to debunk the idea that depression attacks a select group of people or certain types of individuals.

Darkness does not discriminate. It does not concern itself with your skin color nor background. It doesn't care about the level of your education or the depth of your spirituality. The pedigree you possess is the least of its concerns. Your resume doesn't deter it nor distract it from its goal. The shadows want to claim the soul of who you are and its hunger for you is insatiable.

With breath in my lungs, a voice in my throat, and an urgency in my spirit, I won't sit idly by and allow that.

I don't write as one who is specialized in the medical or psychological field, but as one who fights a personal battle while refusing to let others stand alone in theirs. What you are about to read is both my journey through the shadows and what I've done to navigate through them. If you need help going through yours, don't see this book as the complete answer for your situation rather as light in the middle of a dark path. Please reach out to Christ-centered professionals around you who carry both experience and compassion for your mental and emotional health. I do recognize that the severity of my depression and the frequency of it may be considerably different than your experience. That's okay. What really matters is not comparing our pain but recognizing that we all are in this together.

I implore you from the beginning of this book to always remember:

You are not alone.

You have hope.

You can get help.

NATIONAL SUICIDE PREVENTION HOTLINE
1-800-273-TALK
(1-800-273-8255)

INTRODUCTION

Depression has not been a recent development in my life. I've dealt with it for as long as I can remember. When I was younger, nobody talked about it. It wasn't mentioned in school. As a PK (pastor's kid), it really didn't come up at church; if it was spoken of, it was with a heavy stereotype. "Those people" were looked at as individuals you needed to keep your distance from. They were "broken," "unstable," and/or "weird." For me personally, I felt alone. I saw myself as separated from those around me because of what was happening under the surface of my life. It was a struggle. I had not yet developed any techniques to deal with what was happening to me. On top of that, there were no mechanisms at home nor at church to find or get help. The darkness is isolating. Isolation wants to steal hope.

Years of this continued. My coping tactics included eating away my pain and joking things off, and they were no longer working. Throwing myself into my job was no longer helping push away the issue. I felt like I had no one to talk to and questions began to build up.

- Can I talk about this without being stigmatized?
- Who is safe to talk to?
- Will my family, parents, church, and friends be embarrassed if I speak up?
- Will I be broken forever?
- Is there hope for me?

Like many teenagers, I lived in perpetual fear of what people thought about me. From the kids in the neighborhood to the people at church, I chased validation and approval. The idea of letting people down was demoralizing. It would have shattered me to not be liked by people. I found approval as my safe place to hide. That safety, however, came at the price of losing myself. Like a canoe with a hundred leaks, living off people's acceptance as the sole source of joy is a constant, tiring affair. You must constantly seek acceptance or else it will feel like you'll sink into an abyss.

More crucial to me was my feeling I needed the approval of my parents. Their opinion of me was more important than anyone else's. I lived with this lingering fear of disappointing them. To do that would have been devastating. I love them dearly and I've always held them in the highest honor. They have been (and still are) great parents. NOT ONCE have they demanded me to have to "win" their approval. Mom and dad gave me a loving, Christ-centered home. If I had any event to attend, sports or band, at least one of them (if not both) was there. On top of being great parents, they were great pastors. They served people to the nth degree. Generosity is what defines their life.

What does any of this have to do with my depression? Everything. These last few paragraphs have been my attempt to take you "behind the veil" of my upbringing to speak to those who think that emotional darkness is the result of a broken home or devastating past. This was not me. I love my parents and they love my sister and me dearly. However, the condition of your upbringing doesn't qualify or disqualify you from certain struggles. Sometimes life hits you hard regardless of your family background or life resume. The shadows do not care about your depth of faith nor your levels of education. Life is open season for internal storms. The darkness doesn't come to visit; it wants to take up residence.

This was my life. I didn't fully understand depression when I was a teenager nor did I recognize it in my early 20s. Looking back, it would manifest itself in a variety of ways. From having a "down" day of what I assumed was a "bad mood" to a few days of being unable to find joy and meaning in the simple things of life. I remember moments of people asking me to hang out and I'd reply "*no*" as I was torn between zero motivation to be around people and allowing people to see me in the mental state I was in. The shadows would suck any momentum out of me and prevent me from seeing any successes. Name it, from football to friendships to school to my spiritual life, depression seemed to go unaltered. It seems to touch everything; it knows no boundaries.

The more frequent my dark feelings would appear, the heavier the burden of validation felt. I began to battle with worrying that my "condition" was damaging my mom and dad's credibility as parents and pastors. My mind went to the students in my youth group and wondered if they would judge me. Would I be ostracized by my faith community? Unfortunately, I've seen others abandoned by theirs. I didn't want this to happen to me. How can I articulate my feelings so people don't think I've lost my mind? As a natural introvert, I felt like I had only a few very close friends. If they truly knew what I was dealing with, would I find myself isolated from people with no possibility for friendship?

Can you sense the inner turmoil of my teenage mind? The emotional turbulence was wreaking havoc on my life. Depression intends to separate you from others. It longs to isolate you in order to consume you. It grows in the shadows of seclusion. For me, it was succeeding at its job.

What does a good kid do? I became really good at playing the "church" game of putting on my "Christian mask" and doing the things I perceived others expected of me. I did my best to obey my parents and respect authority. I befriended anyone and everyone possible (which earned me the nickname "community Dave" from a friend in high school). While that sounds like the actions of a healthy human being, it actually was an act of desperation. In my mind, perhaps I can convey an image of what people want me to be so they would never know what I was dealing with under the surface. Having a quiet personality, I looked to surround myself with extroverted people so I could hide in the shelter of their charisma and temperament. I hung out with them as they commanded each other's affection and attention. There was no need for me to stand out. I could feel like a "someone" simply by being in proximity to an *actual* "someone."

Don't get me wrong, it wasn't like I had a miserable childhood. There were a ton of great seasons and moments. My family, both immediate and extended, were consistently loving, caring and entertaining. I have a load of fond memories from our single-wide mobile home and that tough neighborhood outside of Detroit. Having never moved until marriage, this neighborhood was all I knew. Thanks to social media, I still have connections with most of the people from my childhood. Along with maintaining connections, the internal challenges continued to linger and grow within me for the next 20 years. From adolescence to adulthood, college to ministry, and marriage to family… I couldn't fathom life without a shadow lurking nearby.

Stepping into my adult life, I felt I had to keep quiet about what I was dealing with. There was no way (in my mind) that I could tell anyone. With the stigma of mental health concerns, I started to question what my future would look like. I mean, who would want to be married to this? Who would want a pastor who weeps over his sermon notes about joy? Who would want to be led by someone who feels this inadequate? Who would want to be seen with a dad that is this emotionally unstable? Eventually, I had reached out to a counselor because my darkness was inviting even darker thoughts. A "doctor's appointment" was my excuse to the church office to cover up my counseling appointments so no suspicions could be raised. I still felt I couldn't tell anyone because the story I told myself, "*Who would want you after they find out what you really deal with internally?*"

Then the events of August 11, 2014 occurred. This was the day the world-renowned actor and comedian, Robin Williams, took his life. I remember the notification coming up on the screen of my phone. What I can only describe as emotional numbness flooded over me from my head to my toes. This icon of comedy, this man of great influence, prominence, and affluence fell prey to the inner darkness that millions of people suffer from.

I'm one of them.

His death hit me hard. I began to ask:

• How does someone with his relational network be subject to something that us "commoners" deal with?

• How is it possible to have seemingly endless resources yet feel like you have no way out?

- How could someone with worldwide notoriety feel so alone?

- How does a human who brought so much laughter to the world live in that depth of inner despair?

For the first time, I understood why suicide rates skyrocket when well-known personalities take their life. Those like me struggling with their own internal turmoil, look at people like Robin, and ask the same questions. Their conclusion can become, "*If he can't make it, I never will either.*"

Something triggered my heart. An overwhelming determination exploded within me. Like a child choosing to stand up to a bully instead of cowering in fear, I could no longer be silent. This was my moment. This was the day that I realized that I couldn't stand on the sideline paralyzed in worry about other people's opinions, quietly watching another life lost while I still had breath in my lungs and a voice to speak.

I sat on my bed and typed my first blog called, "From the Heart of a Depressed Pastor." I typed. I cried. I typed some more. I cried some more. Those 1,029 words I typed that day were covered with four times as many tears. Some of those tears were filled with pain, but if I was really honest, many more of those tears were filled with fear. What was driving my fear?

- I was nervous about what my wife would think. Would this make her feel uncomfortable by having a husband THIS susceptible to depression?

- I feared what my kids would think. Would they be embarrassed of their father?

- I was terrified of what my parents would think. I didn't want to disappoint them nor for them to blame themselves. They were and have always been amazing parents.

- I was concerned about what my congregation would think. At this stage, I had been a Lead Pastor for five years. Would they want me to continue as their pastor? Would the board ask for my resignation?

Most of all, I didn't want to disappoint God. It comes off as ridiculous to think that an omniscient (all-knowing) God would be surprised at anything. Silly as it sounds, there was a voice inside me telling me to keep it to myself because admitting it felt the same as admitting defeat. Speaking out about my struggles could give the Devil victory in my life.

As I typed, the tears flowed but so did the freedom. My heart was beating out of my chest, yet my shoulders began to rise higher in confidence. There is something empowering about standing up to a bully who's lorded over your life. There is something liberating about refusing to succumb to the darkness and choosing to step into the light of God's love. Jesus isn't glorified when you hide your issues. He is honored by us being real with ourselves, real with Him, and placing our hurts into His care. I think of the words of the Psalmist who said, "*Give your burdens to the LORD, and he will take care of you. He will not permit the godly to slip and fall*" (Psalm 55:22 NLT). The Apostle Peter also said, "*Give all your worries and cares to God, for he cares about you*" (1 Peter 5:7 NLT). These words tell me that we not only have the freedom to be real with our "cares," but that Jesus cares for us so much. He encourages us to give them over to Him.

I will tell you my story. It may sound like yours. Although, it may not even begin to scratch the surface of the struggles you are dealing with, if anything, I pray that this book will accomplish four goals.

First, I want to give hope to those who feel alone in the "shadows" of depression. Have you ever felt like the only one who's dealing with this? You know in your head you couldn't possibly be the only one. It's those feelings of isolation unique to your situation that makes the experience feel more exclusive than it really is.

Secondly, I want to help articulate what is difficult to describe. Quite often, those of us in the shadows frustrate others who want to understand what we deal with by not being able to adequately verbalize what we are experiencing. My approach to helping you paint a picture of our shadowy journey is two-fold: The use of personal experiences, and the use of stories from the Scripture. Please know, my use of the biblical narrative is not to manipulate you into thinking all the people mentioned are depressed (even though I truly believe some of them did deal with depression). Accessing these ancient stories can be a tremendous tool to help describe what is being

8

experienced under the surface of our very own lives. Which leads me to the next goal...

Third, I want to shed light on a subject for those of you who've never had to journey through the shadows and to give better insight on what your loved one or friend may be going through. You may not have dealt with depression, but it's real. Nobody who deals with it would truly wish this darkness upon anyone. I pray that this book will help develop a depth of compassion towards those of us who journey through the emotional shadows. My hope is that this book will not just clarify the struggles of others, but also to empower you with the ability to understand and potentially help bring relief and, ultimately, healing.

Lastly, I want to help you to see tomorrow. God has not brought you this far just to bring you this far! Those of us who battle with the shadows, at times, can't envision a single day later, let alone a week, month, or even a year later. I implore you to not allow the depth of the darkness to blind you from a future you have! Life is precious and a gift from God! That means YOU are precious and a gift from God. Reject the notion that you are a "mistake" or "unfixable." Embrace the truth that you are "fearfully and wonderfully made" (Psalm 139:4 ESV), and have a tremendous life ahead of you. True, you may be going through a tough chapter. Please realize, a chapter is not the whole story. It's just a piece of it. There's much more of your story yet to be written.

"Let there be light…"
It's the prayer of everyone who's been hurt by disappointment
When life hits and gives us way more than expected
It's the cry of the overwhelmed heart; the scream of a tired soul
The aching of desperation; fallen deeper into a bottomless hole
But you understand my darkness,
you get the struggle of my inside
So, I lift up my eyes asking you to hear my cry
You hover over my chaos ready to create with just one word
Speak Holy Spirit; I need hope in my hurt
Lord would you speak,
"Let there be light…"

It's the prayer of everyone who feels forgotten
When the devil has convinced them that they're no longer wanted
When he's blinded their eyes from seeing the hope of light
When their strength is drained and unable to get in the fight
I've had victory on the mountain,
but the valley is nothing but distress
Lord it's you I need. I need some hope in my darkness
I call out the only One who can reach into an unreachable place
I know I can find peace if I could just find your face
Lord I need you to speak,
"Let there be light…"

To every person who thought nobody cares
To every tired soul, bearing weights to heavy to bear
To those longing to knock but cannot find the door
To those who seek a way out and cannot take any more
Lift up your face, look beyond the valley.
The sun may have set behind you, but it's not your finale.
There's a God who creates out of the depths of your chaos.
Lift up your head, the Son rises to call to us, "Let there be light…"

- Personal Journal Thoughts

- 1 -

THE TRAUMA OF THE SOUL

"Well, sometimes my life just don't make sense at all
When the mountains look so big,
And my faith just seems so small
So hold me Jesus,
Cause I'm shaking like a leaf
You have been King of my glory
Won't You be my Prince of Peace"

"Hold Me Jesus" by Rich Mullins

"A sound mind makes for a robust body, but runaway emotions corrode the bones."

Proverbs 14:30 MSG

Have you ever been caught off guard by a reaction that came out of you?

A few years ago, I had just pulled out of my garage to head to the office. It was a sunny day so I reached down to grab a pair of sunglasses. I placed them on and realized there was a white spider on the lens. If that wasn't bad enough, the spider was on the INSIDE of the lens, an inch from my eye.

What came out of my lungs was a scream that I'm not sure I could recreate. All I knew at that moment was to throw my glasses as I swerved all around the road, narrowly avoiding the cars parked along the side. Then it occurred to me that the spider was now loose in the car, and I needed to pull over to take care of it. (This had to be a Monday because things like this don't happen any other day of the week.)

I can't say I have a fear of spiders per se, but what has stuck with me years later was the scream that came out of me. It was my unexpected explosive and very dramatic response. I remember thinking about my reaction and saying to myself, "*What was that? Better yet, who was that?*"

This story has always stuck with me as a very simple way to start a dialogue with others about depression. Why? Because I think we've all had moments where what has come out of us has caused us to step back and ask, "*What was that? Better yet, who was that?*"

Maybe the emotions of the moment caught you off guard. Perhaps you are thrown off because something came out of your mouth that you wouldn't normally say in that particular situation. It could be a response you had toward someone who has thrown you for a loop and left you thinking, "*why would I do that?*" Nevertheless, something was triggered, and your reaction has left you puzzled, or worse, wounded.

I bring this up because it was patterns of reactions and responses that caused me to finally reach out and get some help. I'm not saying one or two overreactions equate to being "depressed." Rather, it was a series of moments over the course of my life that threw up multiple red flags. In mathematics it's called the "common denominator." Over the course of my life, I had noticed something was off. Like a wire that's disconnected, everything around me could be fine, yet something heavy and chaotic was happening within me. It wasn't until I was an adult that I realized it wasn't a "personality issue," but an emotional matter at play.

Now, as an adult, I'm pondering a litany of questions about myself. The common denominator wasn't a circumstance; the common denominator was me.

• How could two similar situations produce such different emotional results?

• How could something that is supposed to be enjoyable feel so lifeless?

• How can someone be surrounded by people who genuinely love them, yet feel rejected?

• How can someone sit in a room with hundreds of people and feel so lonely?

• Why can someone see their family thrive yet feel like they've failed them?

• Why does the thought of punishing oneself feel so right, yet bring so much shame?

• Why do people value others' lives more than their own?

This is some of the bedrock of my story. I bet for those of you reading, you resonate with those thoughts (if not personally, you know someone who does). It's a terrible thing to be caught in a trap nobody can see; it is terrifying to be bound by something you struggle to describe. Yet this is the journey none of us asked for. It isn't the life we would wish on anyone else.

But here we are. People living life journeying through the shadows.

"Dave, everyone goes through depression."

I particularly *love* ignorant Facebook comments. After I posted my first blog about depression, my social media began to blow up with comments from people. It confirmed the need for openness about the subject. The responses varied. They ranged from gratitude for my vulnerability to others who felt it provided them with a safe opportunity to admit openly that they deal with depression. My personal messages and email started filling up with people wanting to talk as they've never heard of a pastor dealing with depression. Many, like me, grew up in churches with pastors who projected lives that seemed to be perfect; no issues at all. I'll admit, there is an image we feel pressured to portray; a life of no problems. We feel we need to be strong for others and never show that we, ourselves, have weaknesses or struggles.

A day that I felt emotional liberation began to look like a day of freedom for so many others. The tears of joy flowed throughout the day, seeing people being brave enough to be open with their struggles. Honestly, I really can't remember specific messages or comments, with the exception of one.

Of all people, a long-time friend jumped on my Facebook page to write the words, "**Dave, everyone goes through depression.**" At that moment, I felt demeaned and angry; hurt and resentful. What I read in those five words was, "*Get over it. Everybody deals with it, so quit your crying.*"

This is what depression does. It locked onto that ONE moment, ONE incident, ONE comment amid hundreds of positive and encouraging posts. Depression will find the one small cloud in a 99% clear-sky day. I distinctly remember thinking about deleting my blog and posts. The power of those five words wanted to cripple any progress I had made. On my bed with my laptop in front of me, I remember quieting myself in prayer and writing these words,

"*If despair is the common cold of our emotions, then depression is the cancer.*"

My friend's five words on social media confirmed a genuine concern I have held about the generalization of the word "depression." It's for that reason, when people approach me about their internal struggles, I'll ask them about getting a professional analysis of their situation before they proclaim they are "depressed." In my humble, non-medical opinion, don't speak that word over yourself unless you have sought evaluation and help from a medical professional. To mistakenly use the word "depression," we can do the diagnosis a severe disservice and grow numb to the impact it makes on peoples' lives.

Let's get something out of the way: everyone DOES NOT get/go through/deal with depression, but everyone DOES go through despair. We all have had moments of what I would refer to as sorrow, loss, or even hopelessness. It's a part of being human. Everyone has moments that come in and catch them off guard. What makes depression different from despair is this:

Despair: I feel hopeless (experience).

Depression: I am hopeless (identity).

I've experienced despair much like any human. Despair is a sensation of hopelessness. Like the common cold, it can be caught easily, have a variety of severities, and be diverse in the duration it lasts.

You can *feel* despair...

...if you lost your car keys and you're running late for an important appointment.

...if you forgot to study for a test (like I did in college for my test on Leviticus).

...if your favorite player on your favorite team gets injured.

...if you watch the news.

...if you just lost a close friend or loved one.

Despair is part of the human experience and is a feeling we all can relate to on several levels. It can leave as fast as it came, yet it can stay longer than expected. Most people can experience despair and yet still navigate the normalities of life (job, relationships, friendships, etc.). Just so you understand, I'm not trying to downplay despair nor do I want to treat it lightly, but I think it is necessary to have a distinction between the sensation of despair and the condition of being depressed.

Depression goes much deeper. There is a psychological component that wants to command every fiber of your being so that you transfer a *"feeling"* to an *"identity."* You don't feel *"sorrow as a human being"* as much as you feel like you are a *"sorry version of a human being."* Where despair can have, comparatively, little to no damage or injury to a person, depression is a trauma of the soul. It fractures the foundations of a person, making it difficult to build a life. Why? Because you feel *"less than"* those around you. You live life as if you are always a few steps behind everyone else.

I Feel 50 Paces Behind Everyone

Leprosy is a disease that comes up often in Scripture. It's a condition that affects the nerves and would prevent a person from feeling pain. For example, if someone with leprosy got an injury, the person would not realize it and continue to injure themselves because of their lack of ability to feel pain. It's a terrible way to live; losing the sensation of being able to physically *"feel"* what everyone else feels.

I grew up in the church hearing sermons about these unfortunate individuals in Scripture who had to navigate this terrible disease. It was always emphasized that they couldn't feel pain. That's because most people only think of pain in a very myopic way. People with leprosy may not have nerve endings working correctly, but they still have emotions. They may not have felt pain in their appendages, but they experienced pain in their souls. How may you ask? This terrible sickness caused them to be forced to live on the outskirts of society. Human touch wasn't possible and person-to-person interaction was limited at best. They had to live in isolation from their family, talk to loved ones through a screen, and see their community from a distance.

In the part of the brain that processes pain, a broken arm and the anguish of an emotional injury share a lot of the same circuitry. Even though the neuron patterns in the brain may be a tad different, they are processed in the same area. Why is that an important point? It's so you understand this: pain is pain. And just because lepers can't feel it physically doesn't mean they're not experiencing it emotionally. These people were deteriorating both outwardly and inwardly.

Minimally, a leper was supposed to be 50 paces behind the next healthy human. It's why we see in the biblical story of the "10 lepers who were cleansed" that "*he* (Jesus) *was met by ten lepers, who stood at a distance*" (Luke 17:12 ESV). They were 50 paces off and "*lifted up their voices, saying, 'Jesus, Master, have mercy on us.'*" (Luke 17:12 ESV)

Put yourself in their shoes. There is someone in front of them who is the essence of hope. Help is right in front of them. They notice that others get a chance to see Jesus up close. It seems that those people have a greater chance to be healed because of their proximity to Christ. Because of their condition, these lepers are not allowed anywhere close to him. They can only stand at 50 paces off and call out and hope Jesus hears them.

Can you imagine living life 50 paces behind everyone? This was their reality; their life-sentence. And to make matters worse, some traditions tell us that a leper had to ring a bell calling out "*unclean*" to warn people they were coming. In other words, "*Not only do I have to live with this disease, I also have to announce it to the world everywhere I go.*" What a terrible way to live and what a horrible emotional load to carry.

Life 50 paces behind everyone.

Quite often, I lean on the Scriptures to help paint an image of the feelings and/or experiences of depression. This picture is an accurate description of what distinguishes depression from despair. Despair, you can be surrounded with people to share the load you feel. You can operate in and amongst community with despair. Depression is quite different. It causes you to identify with the isolated feelings so much that it becomes your persona. You feel untouchable and "*unclean.*" It makes you feel as if you are "50 paces behind" everyone else in your life.

50 paces behind the happiness others enjoy.

50 paces behind the peace your friends seem to possess.

50 paces behind what a healthy marriage could be.

50 paces behind being desirable to another human.

50 paces behind the others that seem more suitable for the job you dream of.

50 paces behind the hope you hear preached from a pulpit.

50 paces behind becoming a candidate for healing.

50 paces behind any type of tangible hope.

As a disclaimer: Leprosy and depression are two different conditions, yet I wouldn't wish either condition on anyone. To be honest, I connect well with the lepers and I think you do too. My depression makes me feel as if I'm numb. It makes me walk around feeling "unclean." And the emotional pain is such a load to bear, and the shadows tell you "you have to bear it alone."

He sees me; He steps toward me.

What I am thankful for in this biblical passage is not just an illustration to articulate what my feelings tell me, but I'm given an accurate description of who Jesus is. "*When he saw them...*" (Luke 17:14 ESV) Knowing the scriptures as I do, Jesus was constantly surrounded by crowds of people pushing against him and crying out to him. It would seem that Jesus would only be able to see and hear those healthy people that were in proximity to him. For those of us who feel like there's a chasm between us and God, for those who feel "50 paces" off, Jesus hears us too.

I imagine Jesus turning and pushing through healthy people to get close enough so that these 10 men could hear his voice. Every step toward them invited a variety of responses from the onlookers. The crowd, most likely, stepped back as to get no closer to the "*unclean.*" Those with leprosy, out of the habit of staying distant from healthy human beings probably kept their 50-paced distance. I can totally see Jesus stepping toward them while they start backing up to respect the distance that has been demanded of them. That image alone brings tears to my eyes. There is a Savior who doesn't just see me but he steps toward me in my condition. Even though I may back away, he still is drawn to me.

As a lover of the Psalms, a favorite passage of mine is Psalm 34:18

(NLT), "*The LORD is close to the brokenhearted; he rescues those whose spirits are crushed.*" It tells me that my condition doesn't detour God from coming toward me. My darkness doesn't eliminate me from God's attention. I may feel untouchable and unapproachable, but God is drawn to my brokenness. He is attracted to my condition, not so that he can observe me from a distance, but so that he can participate with me in my hurt. Jesus can meet me in the place of feeling isolated and alone; broken and hopeless. And he comes in to help.

Doing > Feeling

The rest of verse 14 gives us a clue to not only the direction he walked but some instruction he gives. He said to them, "*Go show yourself to the priests.*" (Luke 17:14 ESV)

These simple instructions carry a ton of significance. For this culture, you only show yourself to the priests IF you are healthy so that they can confirm you are healthy. When Jesus spoke, I honestly don't believe they were healed in that exact moment. Why? Verse 15 clues us in with seven words.

> "*And as they went they were cleansed.*"
> (Luke 17:15 ESV)

Jesus gave them some direction. It was a simple action for them to take that would have been contrary to what their feelings would have told them. And that, my friends, is a huge part of working through depression. "Doing" trumps "feelings." It's about making moves "*against the grain*" of your emotions. It's taking a stand in your life by acting upon what is right even though the darkness whispers to do otherwise.

The healing for these 10 men was tied to their actions. They needed a response congruent, not with their emotions, but to what they knew was the healthy direction. The instructions were simple, yet the task wasn't easy. There was risk involved. Why? Because in this culture, you were not healed of leprosy unless the priests confirmed your healing. To "*go show yourself to the priests*" with the hopes that you were healed only to have them pronounce the words "*unclean*" would have been devastating. Jesus said, "*go*" and they must have looked at each other thinking, "*but nothing has changed yet.*"

This is part of the internal conflict for those of us living in the shadows of depression. It's the ongoing battle of doing what we KNOW is healthy versus doing what we FEEL like in the moment (and we'll dig deeper into that in another chapter).

For these 10 men, their healing came on the other side of their obedience. Their freedom was experienced when they decided to move from their dark place, not because it felt right, but because it was right.

"And as they went..."

Sometimes the best thing to do is to move; to be actively pursuing healthy responses to the inner darkness. For these men, the only way for them to make any progress with their condition was to go back to the ones who, most likely, pronounced them "*unclean.*" This therapeutic direction by Jesus was more than just to get them to be healed on the outside but to confront some of their internal issues. These men were physically ostracized, 50 paces behind everyone else. As we've emphasized, they were also ostracized emotionally, mentally, and spiritually. And the sight of a priest would have been a reminder of this. Jesus' instructions bring the men face to face with their internal trauma, not to make them uncomfortable but to make them whole. Sometimes we avoid traumatic moments and people because we don't want to get hurt again. Jesus sends them to the priests so that they can hear the words that will heal their soul, "*You are clean.*"

To see change, you need to recognize that anything external must be dealt with internally. Jesus' direction for these men was just that. Their skin needed to be healed, but so did their soul. They needed to be cleansed of leprosy physically, but they also needed to be restored on the inside. We have to take in account that sometimes the healing we desire comes in the form of us intentionally making healthy movements forward instead of waiting for someone to do things for us. The acceptance, the peace, the friendships, the community...all *can* come from people initiating relationships with us. Often, what we are looking for comes from us being the ones to make the movements toward, not what we *feel* is right but what we know is healthy.

I believe today is a new day for you. It's a day to stop listening to the voice of the darkness saying, "*You can never be whole; you'll never find healing. You will always live 50 paces behind the rest of the world.*" Depression is a liar and will try to convince you that this is a life sentence. Today is the first day of a new day for you. I believe this will be a moment when you'll begin to see the sun rising where night was all you could see. Today is a day where you will detect hope where it seemed impossible to find it. Today is your day to make some intentional decisions to move forward to get the help and the health you deserve.

You're no longer 50 paces behind.

You are now one step ahead of where you were. And tomorrow, you'll be one more pace further than today.

Survival Tips for the Shadows:
The Survival Rule of 3

Going into the woods alone invites challenges. Not only do you have no one to help, but if something were to happen, nobody would know. Because of that, there is something called the "Rule of 3." These are 3 trusted individuals in your life that know you and know what you are about to embark upon.

It's simple. You contact your "3" and let them know:

• Where are you going? Location, coordinates, etc.

• When are you leaving? Give them the exact time and day.

• When are you returning? Again, give them the exact time and day.

Upon return, your job is to simply call the "3" to let them know you're safe.

I know it sounds simple, but the "Rule of 3" has immense importance. If you do not call your "3" back when you return, they know that something is wrong, and you are in danger. This group is now responsible to contact any rescue and recovery entities and give them your last known whereabouts. The "Rule of 3" is your lifeline in case of the unexpected happening in your isolation.

One of strategies for navigating the shadows of depression is the "Rule of 3." These are 3 friends who not only know me, but they also have experienced the shadows. When the darkness rises in my life, my call goes out to these three. If they don't hear from me after that call, they immediately reach out to me to check in on me to see how I'm doing. This group has saved my hope and brought me strength in the darkest of times.

Who are your 3? Who can you entrust your emotional life with to support you, pray for you, listen to you, and call in to check on you? Pray. Make your list. Tell them what you expect. Contact them and ask them to be part of your "Survival Group of 3." If they agree, the next time you venture into a shadowy season, you can contact them and not navigate the shadows alone.

- 2 -

THE CHURCH AND THE STIGMA

I've carried a burden
For too long on my own
I wasn't created
To bear it alone
My heart needs a surgeon
My soul needs a friend
So I'll run to the Father
Again and again and again.

"Run to the Father" by Cody Carnes

"He heals the brokenhearted and binds up their wounds."

Psalm 147:3 NLT

Did you grow up with any stereotypes in your schools and/or neighborhoods? I did. I know they are not "truths" at all but they're only as accurate as my teenager's emotional memory recalls. Isn't that what stereotypes do? They give generalized labels to groups of people based on a couple examples. Here's a few that I grew up with:

- Jocks (specifically football players) were dumb.
- Blondes were absent minded.
- People with tattoos were dangerous and could not be trusted.
- If you smoked, you were called a "burnout" and were considered to possess little worth.
- Smart kids were nerds and band kids are geeks.
- Goths were dangerous and should be avoided.
- Preppies (nicely dressed) were arrogant because people assumed they came from families of affluence.
- Skaters were rebellious and a bad influence.
- People from the local trailer park were both trouble and *troubled*.

Can you tell I was an 80's kid? I'd love to say that the stereotypes and stigmas ended in my childhood, but they continue. Even today, I feel stereotyped because of my tattoos. As mainstream as they've become, I get stigmas spoken to me as a pastor.

"You must have gotten those before you became a Christian."

"Do you have a troubled past?"

"You must be a liberal pastor."

"You know, you don't have to do that to try to be cool."

It seems that people tend to place labels on others for two reasons: First, they often label what they do not understand. Why? It's much easier to label someone to define them for our minds sake instead of getting to know the person behind the label. For example, being from the local trailer park, I had classmates label me a stupid and inept because I didn't live in a home like they did. They had one or two bad interactions with someone from my neighborhood and the rest of us living there got stereotyped. Looking back in my past at the categories and stigmas used on people, if you made any effort to get to know them, you may discover:

• Many, if not most, of my football teammates achieved academic honors.

• Hair color and piercings had nothing to do with intellect or awareness.

• Tattoos are about self-expression and not about threat.

• Whether you smoke or not, you are of extreme worth.

• "Nerd" and "geek" are often used as a compliment to someone's intelligence.

• "Goths" have been some of the kindest individuals I know.

• Arrogance isn't dictated by a clothing label.

• Skaters wouldn't feel the need to be rebellious if you didn't try to chase them off all the time.

• Some people from the trailer park grow up, become pastors, and write books on depression.

People love to label so they don't have to connect. This leads me to my second point. People label to achieve a sense of control. Let's be real, this goes far beyond teenagers stereotyping each other but we adults do it too. We carry this type of thinking from the adolescent into our adulthood. Why? If I label you, I can control your narrative in my mind. I can stuff you into a category and leave you there. We do this to neighbors. We do this to coworkers. We do this to family. We do it because there's less responsibility for people who are in specific categories. Labels give you permission to keep your distance so that "other people" can deal with them.

It's bad enough to know that this takes place in schools, neighborhoods, and the workplace. Unfortunately, stereotyping has infiltrated the Church. I've heard comments from church members and sermons from preachers who either don't understand or refuse to try to grasp what affects millions of people around our world. I've been told that depression is:

• A spiritual condition with nothing to do with the physical or mental.

• An issue of sin.

• An act of God's judgment.

• The refusal to have faith in Christ.

• No different than having a bad day.

• Something you can change by deciding to cheer up.

Friends, it's time to wake up and get educated. It's time to realize that if depression is not in your scope, it doesn't lessen the impact it has on others. I've heard it said, *"I've got Jesus and I've never been depressed."* My friend, count yourself blessed for that. If you'd look at the Scriptures closely, you'd notice there are a ton of VERY human people who were used mightily by God but navigated some very dark seasons. To name a few, people like Moses, Elijah, Naomi, Hannah, and David dealt with dark seasons but are held in very high regard. Even the man whom Jesus called the greatest prophet, John the Baptist, sat in a literal prison dealing with internal darkness and doubt. We have to recognize that internal darkness is real. It can hit anyone, even those of us in the Church.

So, if you don't know or worse, refuse to learn, then you are going to hurt those around you and miss opportunities to help people, and even create unsafe atmospheres in the Church that could make people think it's safer to stay in the shadows than to step into the light. This sends people back into isolation to deal with it on their own which is the last thing a broken soul needs.

A broad brush with only one can of paint

Back in 2018, a tweet was sent out by a world-renowned pastor about the subject of depression. He said,

"Depression is a result of spiritual starvation. Overcome depression and emotional hardships by immersing yourself in God's Word."

I really try hard not to do angry social media responses. (Truth be told, I'm really challenged with this while I'm watching the Detroit Lions.) Why don't I "get into it" with people on these platforms? It's because I don't want my social media presence defined by angst and bitterness. My heart isn't to be a part of what's wrong with this medium but part of the solution to what we can do with it. What I've done is create a simple rubric for which I filter all my social media. So, before I post or respond, I ask:

- Will it inspire a mind?

- Will it build a heart?

- Will it bring a smile?

That said, I've typed out quite a few angry posts and responses that were followed by either the delete button (or more likely my wife talking me down from the social media ledge and having me back away from commenting all together). There are a ton of draft blogs I've written out of hurt and anger that have never been posted. Though they were therapeutic to write them out, it would have been destructive to post them. *"But Dave, shouldn't you say how you feel?"* I'll say in a concise way, NO. Saying how we feel to blow off steam at the expense of taking the time to process what we are feeling can give momentary relief but involves long-term repercussions.

On this particular day, I didn't hold back. My response (now deleted) to this well-known minister came out of the hurt I had incurred from other church people and leaders who, out of ignorance or the refusal to educate themselves, have inflicted pain and fracture on others for no other reason than to sound spiritual all the while leaving a trail of devastation. Can spiritual starvation be a *trigger* to depression? Sure. Can spiritual starvation *feed* depression? Absolutely.

However, to simplify the cure for depression down to simply reading the Bible is dangerous. To chalk depression up to nothing more than a spiritual condition, without weighing the physical and emotional health of the individual, is harsh, negligent, and harmful.

From my personal experiences, the Church has used a broad brush dipped in one color to paint a portrait of depression. Although, there are of course informed and energized individuals, the Church as a whole seems to be behind the times on this particular topic. I know pastors who've distanced themselves from the psychological community out of some thought that sending people to clinicians as less spiritual than sending sick people to a doctor. This I don't understand. You approve of people in your church going to a physician but not a Christ-centered psychologist? Why? Some of it may be a disagreement with the whole industry of counseling and therapy. I know of one pastor who told me that sending people to therapists was "demonic" as the whole industry was founded by an atheist. If that's the case, we'd better take inventory over everything we use in life to see if Christians invented, built, modeled, etc. everything we use on an everyday basis.

I think a big part of pastors not partnering with clinicians is control. *"Why would I send people away to get what I can give them? These are my sheep and I'm their shepherd. I know what's best for them."* To that I'd say, first, that you at best are an under-shepherd and your congregation are sheep of God's pasture. He is the Great Shepherd. Second, as an under-shepherd, your responsibility is stewardship of the people you serve. If you are not properly trained or equipped to deal with deep inner hurt and mental illness, you need to position your people to get the healthy direction they need and they may not come from you.

To every pastor reading this book, PLEASE recognize that you are not personally equipped to meet EVERY need of your congregation! That's impossible. I know you want to believe you are, or worse, that you should be able to bear everyone's load. You cannot serve every need. To think or live that way will destroy your ministry as you'll work tirelessly doing things you shouldn't be doing in the first place. You'll spend too much time struggling with situations that could be handled more efficiently and more effectively by a more qualified professional which will lead to healthy and revitalized lives. You could be mishandling situations because of your lack of appropriate education and expertise in this area. Please understand, we already have our Savior, so you don't have to be everyone else's savior. Be fearless about admitting that it may just be in your parishioner's best interest to refer them out for therapy with a licensed Christ-centered provider.

Please meet with your local counselors. Take them out to coffee. Get to know their hearts and their specialties. See that they are on your side and that they are a tremendous gift to the Kingdom of God. I have a policy that says I will NEVER recommend a local counselor that I have not met in person. I want a relationship with those helping bring healing into the people I serve.

As I often say: It's not a weakness to ask for help. It's a weakness to *not* ask for help.

Pastors, that means you too. If you have people in your congregation who are beyond your expertise, humbly admit it to them and give them a few recommendations for a couple clinicians that could help breathe health into them. Healthy congregation members won't see that as a weakness in you. They'll see your referral as a strength of character, a safe relationship, and a Kingdom heart. They will respect you for it and even recommend others to seek your counsel. Why? You loved them enough to take the focus off of you and give them a direction that facilitates the help and healing they need.

"It's just another issue they have."

Depression is a mental, emotional, and medical illness. Yet in the Church, we make it about issues we can "explain away" or handle. Why do we do that? Partially, it's ignorance. I think the other part of it goes back to control; explaining the issue in a way that puts the power back into my hands. This is the reason, I feel, why people in the church have traditionally described depression as:

• A "*circumstantial*" issue: "*They wouldn't feel like this if it wasn't for the circumstances.*" Circumstances can certainly trigger depression. A multiplicity (layers) of circumstances can in fact invite it in. This approach is about trying to explain the depression to the point that says, "*If I can fix their situation, I will fix them.*"

• A "*faith*" issue: "*If you just had more faith (like me), then you wouldn't feel this way.*" What seems like a well-intended suggestion actually has the opposite effect. While my mind knows I have faith, my feelings are telling me I don't. When somebody "spiritual" comes in to tell me what I don't have, it confirms what the darkness is telling me. The depressed mind hears, "*If I had faith, I wouldn't struggle like this.*"

• A "*sin*" issue: "*What did you do (sin committed) to bring this upon yourself?*" Can sin invite darkness? Absolutely. In my experience, when sin is brought up, it isn't necessarily to help understand the person but to confirm the suspicion they have about the other's depression. "*That's what I thought. I knew it was sin that caused it.*"

• A "*consequential*" issue: "*Welp, I bet this happened because he or she did _____ to deserve it.*" Like the "*sin issue,*" this is a cynical approach to understanding the person by finding their own diagnosis in order to cast judgment. Let's be real, consequences from decisions can invite the darkness in. Those decisions don't have to be wrong or sinful. Sometimes we live in the wake of the ramifications of other people's decisions which have little to no reflection on any of our own choices. Look deeper. Stay away from starting with, "*What did you do to cause this? You should stop doing that.*"

• A "*decision*" issue: "*You need to take a step of faith and decide to not be depressed.*" What's wild is to think that anyone would "decide" to be depressed. Who would? We don't want this, nor would we wish it on anyone. We are not "doing this" for attention. By the way, if it was a matter of the will, we'd be done with it forever. The hyper-faith movement has turned to "decision-based faith actions" as our answer to life's challenges we conceal. We don't need Jesus as much as we need to be the one who sets ourselves free with our own decisions. If you're hearing, "*you are choosing to stay depressed,*" please find a new Christ-centered friend to confide in. You should feel supported, not guilted, when discussing such a sensitive and painful topic.

• An "*insignificant*" issue: "*I've never had to deal with that, and I've been around a long time.*" This approach is one of the most hurtful because, unless the listener has had any experience or interaction with the issue of depression, it really isn't a legitimate or real issue in their mind. Not only does it come off as callous, but it rallies other people to begin to think the same way. My take: This thinking is fear-based. *"I don't know how to deal with an unfamiliar issue, so instead of investigating, I will delegitimize the person and their experience."* Life outside of their purview doesn't exist, therefore, no action is needed until they go through a similar experience and someone makes them feel this way.

• A *"comparative"* issue: *"I went through the same things as that person, and I was fine."* Have you ever seen two people go through the same situation yet be impacted differently? One comes out seemingly unscathed while the other seems devastated; unable to recover. For the first individual, if they're fine after the moment, it seems everyone else should be too. This happens often with parents and their children. Parents often forget that even though our kids are like us, they are not us and have to process their own experiences when they occur. They have distinct personalities even though they have similar genetics. Be careful with, *"I was fine. You should be too."* You may have made it through your journey without so much as a struggle. Don't downplay it if others are experiencing more challenges than you did.

• A *"weakness"* issue: *"If you are dealing with this, it's because you haven't matured yet in that area."* This has such a close connection to the *"comparative issue"* with the big difference being the subject of the statements. In the *"comparative issue,"* "I" is the subject (look at me), whereas in the *"weakness issue,"* "you" is the subject (look at you). These people love to lay out how your lack of strength is what is leading you into depression. *"You're going to have to grow strong and improve yourself so as to not allow this to happen again."*

• A *"conspiracy"* issue: *"The reason why this is happening so often today is because of all of the antidepressants being over-prescribed."* What these people are really saying: Your mental illness isn't real; it's the product of Big Pharma, the Government, or some other entity they've decided to blame. They'll rail against medications they don't agree with and be fine with the medications they approve of (if they approve of any at all). They will be okay with getting medical help for other things, but mental health, that's more of a product of your own imagination. *"You don't have mental health issues. It's a ploy to control your life. You can do this without any help."*

• A "*faith-testing*" issue: "*What you are feeling is God's way of testing you and your faith.*" Does God test us? Yes. Does God in His sovereignty allow trials to come our way? Absolutely. Yet, to throw out a blanket statement like this without any knowledge of the person nor the situation is spiritually abusive. I don't believe that depression IS the trial. I think depression can be something we experience as a RESULT of the trial. "*God doesn't give us more than we can handle.*" Not true. What in life does God give us that we were meant to be able to handle by ourselves? We are supposed to rely on Him in all things and to lean into community for one another for support.

We, the Church, need to push our ignorance, bias, and misunderstandings aside to get a grip on both what we've missed and what we can now do for those suffering with depression. These hurting individuals need our presence more than they need our commentary; they need hope more than our judgment. It's time for us, the Church, to get into a place where our normative response is different from our historical response. It's time to change our narrative.

We need to find our groove

My guess is some of you have navigated through similar waters when it comes to mental illness and the Church. Personally, I come from a charismatic tradition, so I've seen all sorts of amplified versions of these approaches to dealing with people living in the shadows.

"*If you had more of the Spirit…*"

"*If you would get your eyes on Jesus…*"

"*Have you used your authority as a believer? If you did, then…*"

Don't get me wrong, I love my pentecostal upbringing and would still describe myself as pentecostal. I refuse to slam my tradition because of some mistakes that have been made. Let's be real, all our Christian traditions have made mistakes (and will continue to make them if human beings are involved. It's human nature!). Yes, I tend to show grace because I believe that should be the starting place. When it comes to enacting our own Christian traditions, we need to be constantly cautious that we are not creating barriers to people and their mental health struggles! We should be in the business of building bridges to get to them. We need a new *modus operandi*; we need a new groove.

One of the most underestimated animated films of all time is Disney's 2000 film called "*The Emperor's New Groove.*" I remember buying it reluctantly because our kids were sick of the DVDs we were traveling with. So I spent $5 and we bought what quickly became a family favorite. In the first part of the movie, an older man was thrown out of a window for throwing off the Emperor's "groove"

"*His what?*"

"*His groove! The rhythm in which he lives his life. His pattern of behavior. I threw it off.*"

We, the Church, need a new groove. Historically speaking, our reputation as the global Church isn't great for handling depression. How do I know? First, I'd say my personal experience growing up in the church world. I'm not just a pastor, but I'm a fourth-generation ministerial credential holder (i.e. I'm a PK or a "pastor's kid"). I don't say that to boast, but to prove a simple point: I grew up in church. My family has for four generations. Therefore, I know the Church world well. Second, from the countless conversations I have with all walks of people. I have been privy to those who've been mishandled by ignorance and discrimination; affected by isolation and rejection. They were left alone when they were reaching out for Christ-like compassion. Even today, other pastors will message me requesting to have confidential conversations because they need to talk but have a fear of losing their positions or credentials if their congregations or supervising ministers hear about their struggles. What that tells me is that from the top to the bottom, both pastors and congregation members are struggling with depression, and nobody knows what to do about it. Depression doesn't just attack those living in sin. It sinks its fangs in the righteous as well.

We need a new groove. We need a new pattern of behavior. Where does the fault lie? Honestly, I really don't know, nor do I care. I'm just done with "*thoughts and prayers*" about the issue. It's time to roll up our sleeves and be involved in doing something to help those afflicted find and receive healing.

We in the church have to do better. We must do better. We are losing lives and losing souls.

The **first step** to the church getting a new groove in overcoming the stigma of depression is to educate ourselves and others about the facts of mental illness. Let me give you some 2020 stats according to the National Alliance on Mental Illness (NAMI),

• Here in the United States, nearly 1 in 5 adults experience some degree of mental illness each year. That means somewhere around 48.8 million adults experiencing mental illness in a calendar year.

• Nearly 1 in 25 adults (10 million people) live with a serious mental illness.

• One half of all chronic mental illnesses begin by the age of 14. Three quarters develop by the age of 24.

• Depression is the #1 leading cause of disability world-wide.

• Serious mental illness costs America $193.2 billion in lost earnings annually.

• 90% of those who die due to suicide had an underlying mental illness. Suicide is the 10th leading cause of death in the United States.

We have an epidemic of massive proportions that we (the Church) cannot continue to turn a blind eye to. Take these stats and apply them to your church. Think about 1 in 5 people that sit in your Sunday services. Think about 1 out of every 5 people sitting in your pew with you. Don't tell me people with mental illnesses don't come to church. Many times, church is where they come for warmth and guidance in times of internal darkness. Are we aware of these hurting souls? Are we prepared to minister to them?

One of the reasons why I suffered in silence in my personal struggle with depression is because of the stigma that continues to remain on those of us who fight the shadows. As a pastor, in my brain, who would want me to be their shepherd? What church would want to hire me if they knew my struggle? What denomination or fellowship would give me credentials?

Back in 2019, I was going through an incredibly dark time to the point that I was dealing with suicidal images. I got help. I sought counsel. After getting help, I reached out to the minister who oversees our denomination in our state. He was shocked and I think a bit hurt that I didn't reach out to him beforehand. I should have. I've known him for 30 years. I looked him directly in the eye and said, *"I know you. I trust you. I don't trust the office or the position and I don't know how to change that mentality."* I'm very thankful for his encouragement and leadership. I'm grateful for his patience and his listening ear. My goal that day wasn't to shame him but to help pull back the curtain for others like me who want help but feel they're going to sacrifice their callings and positions because of the depression they are facing.

The stigmas connected to the ignorance about mental illnesses STILL linger in many of our churches. The silence of our pulpits, the uninformed and/or insensitive statements made by congregants, and the lack of education on mental health maintenance is causing believers to feel shamed, blamed, and very unsupported. What that results in is a ton of outstanding Christ-centered individuals who suffer in the shadows, silent and alone.

This leads me to my **second step** for churches: become a safe, healthy community. This can mean any number of things. Talk about depression in the pulpit. Create spaces in your small groups where the subject can be dialogued. Share testimonies about mental health challenges. Encourage people to get help from the medical community (people need to see that their church doesn't take a stand against doctors and medications). Make the subject the normative for your congregation rather than the taboo subject nobody wants to admit is happening. Invite local counselors to teach a few classes to give your adults exposure to mental health challenges. Offer prayer support for those who are struggling. Have an ethos amongst church leadership that shows gratitude and genuine kindness to those who share their struggles. As a church, you can't do everything, but adopting the philosophy that *everybody* can do *something* will help meet people who suffer in the shadows.

The scenario makes me think of one of the most well-known stories shared in Scripture. It was a story Jesus told. Oftentimes, Jesus would tell parables in which simple stories used to convey deep spiritual truths to His listeners. It was in Luke 10 where Jesus shared this world-renowned story about a man who was on a journey and fell prey to a group of bandits who stripped him, beat him, and left him for dead. Nothing about the story would have shocked the audience. This was normal. These things happened on the road between cities.

What happened next is what began to stir the pot.

Jesus tells of two separate people, at separate times, walking by and seeing the beaten and broken man. These two men were known as a "Priest" and a "Levite." In our western world, we can translate that to a Pastor and a church leader. These two who studied what God expected, knew the love of God, and did their best to make sure their lives were acceptable to the Lord, did just the opposite that day. They saw the man and passed right by without a single thought of what to do about him. If they had any thoughts, there was certainly no outward expression. If there's anything this story should remind us is that any small actions of kindness is more powerful than the greatest intentions. At best, these two church workers had some thoughts and prayers thrown toward this broken man. That's it.

Jesus stirs the pot some more.

He tells of a third man that came along. For the Jewish audience listening to Jesus' story, they're waiting for the hero of the story to emerge. What they didn't expect was for the man to be a Samaritan. A Samaritan was of mixed descent. Half Jewish, half Gentile this race was despised by both the Jewish race and the Gentile race. The product of an interracial marriage, a Samaritan lived knowing what it was like to be ignored and hated simply because of his heritage mixed of two lineages. Yet when he saw another human hurting, all he could feel was compassion; the need to care for someone in need.

This Samaritan didn't care about genetics. He didn't ask where the man went to church. He didn't even inquire if he even believed in God. His help was not contingent on him being allowed to lead this man through the "sinner's prayer." He didn't make the broken man make any promises or commitments to anything nor did he ask for anything in return. This Samaritan saw a human whose life he had the ability to impact. He didn't ponder the implications nor did he take the easy way out by walking by. Simply said: He saw a need; he met a need.

In sermons and teachings, we've always pointed our fingers at the Priest and Levite to toss blame on them as humans. We have to go deeper. There's something very sobering about thinking about who these two represent. It's us, the Church. There are people who are beaten up and broken emotionally. Unfortunately, some have had their church leadership pass them by, thinking that helping people with mental issues is someone else's burden. Some have had congregation members ignore them hoping someone else will come along and invest their time and efforts, as it seems easier to ignore than to invest in the stories of the brokenhearted.

Years ago, I had seen an old picture of a church in Germany stationed near a railroad track. The story behind it was that during the days of Nazi Germany, when the church would hold services, trains pulling cars full of Jews on their way to concentration camps would go by, making a lot of noise. The minister would tell the congregation to "sing louder" to overcome the sound of the train and its cargo. Why? If they don't notice, they wouldn't feel compelled to take responsibility.

We can't be the church that continues to sing loud and pray hard but refuse to act. We need the Church to become "Samaritans" who will take notice and do something. We need a church willing to step out of the mode that has made us "walk on by" hurting and broken people and invest our time, abilities, and yes, even our finances. With the stats we are seeing on mental health and suicide, we cannot afford to wait. Today is the day to start noticing. Today is the day to stop being intentionally uninformed and to do something about your brothers and sisters who are hurting in emotional despair.

Turning a blind eye isn't an option for us, the Church. We are to be the new generation of "Samaritans" who cannot pass by. We are to be the first to respond. We need to be the "tip of the spear" of people who are willing to engage those living in the shadows to be exactly what Christ called us to be: a light in the darkness.

"Here's another way to put it: You're here to be light, bringing out the God-colors in the world. God is not a secret to be kept. We're going public with this, as public as a city on a hill. If I make you light-bearers, you don't think I'm going to hide you under a bucket, do you? I'm putting you on a light stand. Now that I've put you there on a hilltop, on a light stand—shine! Keep open house; be generous with your lives. By opening up to others, you'll prompt people to open up with God, this generous Father in heaven.

Matthew 5:14-16 MSG

Survival Tips for the Shadows:
Don't Quit

In 1952, a woman named Florence Chadwick decided to attempt the 26-mile swim between the California coastline and Catalina Island. During her swim Florence traveled with a team whose job it was to keep an eye out for sharks and be prepared to assist in the event of unexpected cramps, injury, or fatigue.

Roughly 15 hours into her swim a thick fog began to set in, clouding Florence's vision and confidence. Her mother happened to be in one of the boats at the time as she heard her daughter relay to the team that she didn't think she could complete the swim.

Florence attempted to swim for another hour before deciding to call it quits. As she sat in the teetering boat trying to recover, she looked up and discovered that if she'd continued on for another mile, she would have reached Catalina Island.

When your depression creeps in to fog your vision of where you are going and what you can accomplish, don't give up.

- Get help.
- Go outside for a walk.
- Pray.
- Find an enjoyable activity.
- Call a friend.

Do any or all of that. Get creative with how to clear your mind and your soul.

But don't give up.

Why? In Christ, the best has yet to come.

- 3 -

THE STRESS-FRACTURE OF THE SOUL

You bring life to the barren places
Light to the darkest spaces
God, it's Your nature
You bring joy to the broken hearted
Hope to the ones who've lost it
God, it's Your nature

"Your Nature" by Kari Jobe

"Even though troubles came down on me hard, your commands always gave me delight. The way you tell me to live is always right; help me understand it so I can live to the fullest."

Psalm 119:143-144 MSG

I'm always honored to be given a chance to give talks outside of the church I serve. For a kid who grew up introverted, public speaking has gone from something I would dread to an event I look forward to. One invitation was particularly exciting because it was taking me to downtown Detroit, the heart of the city I grew up in. I remember taking my son with me on that occasion to introduce him to the city that was so near and dear to my heart.

We drove all over Detroit. We went to the downtown stadiums and stopped at the Hockeytown Cafe as we both are Red Wing fans. Of course, we had to get coney dogs (that's a chili dog for non-Michiganders) from each of the dueling side-by-side restaurants Lafayette Coney Island and American Coney Island because that's what you do for lunch in "the D" (I lean towards Lafayette's chili).

When we were done with our tour of the Detroit attractions, I got out my phone and opened up my GPS to find the location I was speaking at. The venue we were heading to was in a part of downtown that I wasn't familiar with. We arrived at our location with time to spare to meet up with our host, enjoy dinner, and finish out the evening by speaking to a roomful of students who were spending a better part of their week showing compassion to Hispanic children and families in a part of Detroit known as "Mexican Town."

The night went great up until the point when we needed to head home. I pulled out my phone to use the GPS app again and my phone began to act peculiar to say the least. Without me touching the screen, it appeared to act as if it had a mind of its own as it began to navigate itself in and out of other apps. The screen was swiping left and right by itself. Apps were starting randomly and then closing on their own. When I tried to select an app, my phone quickly chose a number at random out of my contacts list and started calling them, only to hang up a few seconds later. This caused people to try calling me back only to have my phone hang up on them yet again.

My problem here was that I needed to get home and my only GPS was on my malfunctioning phone. This was just beyond the years of when we carried physical maps in our glove boxes. So with my phone malfunctioning, I had no other resources to guide me out of this area. My son and I were left to sit in a dark car in downtown Detroit wondering how to find our way back to Kalamazoo. After continuously selecting my GPS app (and ignoring who my phone was attempting to call), we somehow got the map working and got ourselves headed in the direction of home. Keep in mind, if you are not from the midwest, you may not understand how serious parts of downtown Detroit can get after dark.

The next day, I called up customer care and they used a term I had not heard of: *Self-navigating*.

My phone acted in a way contrary to what was "normal." Instead of allowing the user to be *in command*, the phone "*self-navigated*" all of my apps and features without my involvement. Physically, there weren't cracks or outside damage. There wasn't even a scuff mark. But on the interior, something was "off." Perhaps something happened that caused the damage. Perhaps I got one of those random phones that come off the assembly line in imperfect working order, and decided that being in downtown Detroit was the exact moment to begin malfunctioning. To this day, I don't really know what happened. All I know is that something happened inside the device that caused it to act in a way that kept me from using it for any normal function.

This has become my way of describing what people can experience when it comes to emotional struggles.

You don't see bruises.

You don't see scrapes.

You can't see a cast or a bandage.

You can't tell with the naked eye that something is wrong.

You can't detect any issues on the outside because the problems at hand have very little to no connection to what is happening on the inside. Everything may look fine outwardly, but inwardly, your emotions are self-navigating all over the place.

"You okay?"

I'm willing to believe there are a few people reading this book that have lived through a similar circumstance, not necessarily with their phones, but in their depression. On the outside, everything *looks* put together. Nothing *seems* wrong or out of balance about their lives…but on the inside, something is "off"; something isn't working like we think it should. On the surface, life *looks* like "clear skies and sunshine." Internally, however, emotions and thoughts are self-navigating all over the place causing a variety of responses. Tears unexpectedly fill our eyes in seemingly random moments. Terrible phrases will roll off our tongues that we didn't expect to say. Dreadful thoughts flow through our minds like a flash flood.

As this happens, friends and coworkers will stare in wonderment and say,

"You don't look like anything is wrong."

"You seemed fine a minute ago."

"You don't seem yourself."

"You need to appreciate the life you have."

"Other people have it worse."

"When you get your act together, then come talk to me."

"Why don't you just tell me what's wrong?"

I think I can speak on behalf of those of us living in the shadows when I say first and foremost that you cannot judge a book by its cover. I know it's an old cliché, but it fits so well for those battling depression. It is rare for a depressed soul to outright wear their pain publicly. We attempt to put up a front to protect people from our darkness, but also to protect ourselves from being hurt even more deeply. Our mentality tells us we have to deal with this on our own to make sure we don't inflict others with our inner pain. Conveniently, this allows us to continue guarding our own hearts from people hurting us in our vulnerable position.

Secondly, to those who have expressed concern for us, we want you to know that if we thought we could, we would tell you what's wrong if we knew how to articulate it. Many times, we don't know exactly what the issue is or what triggered it. All we know is something isn't *right* on the inside. Don't be fooled. We may *look* put together on the outside, but it doesn't mean we are actually doing okay. Don't be misled by the masks we sometimes wear. When the depression is at lower levels, we are able to "suit up" for a moment in order to deflect any unwanted attention. Rather than enduring yet another "concerned" individual who genuinely wants to help but is clueless as to how, we act our way through work, church, family functions, etc. We are able to sometimes wear a smile through a meeting or an event, but at the end of the day, we collapse on our beds completely exhausted from enduring one more day of putting up a front, while our emotions self-navigate all over the place.

We'd love to stop the roller coaster of emotions, but that means we would need to identify what is going on internally. Most of the time, I prefer to not use the work "broken," but instead prefer the word "fractured."

Why?

When people think "broken," there tends to be little to no hope. A fracture creates possibilities. With a fracture, there's still somewhat of a connection.

Stress-fractured, not stress-broken

Have you ever had a stress fracture? Years ago, when I began running, shoes were rarely on my list of necessities. I decided to buy a pair that looked good but were actually not good to run in. The cost: a stress fracture in my foot. So for the next few weeks, I had to deal with a pain that could have been avoided had I bought shoes that were not just made for running, but that could endure the miles I was putting on.

Nowadays, I switch up my shoes when I've gotten the recommended mileage out of them. It's become one of the reasons I use an app to keep track of the miles on my shoes. After 500 miles, I "retire" the shoes and run in a new pair. Over time and use, shoes lose the support they once had which can cause undue stress on feet, ankles, and knees. When people ask me about running, they'll often talk about foot problems which tend to flare up while they run, or shortly thereafter. They don't realize they either didn't buy the proper shoes or they need to get out of the overused pair they've owned and are still using. They don't understand how much undue stress they're putting on their legs because they haven't changed up their shoes.

A stress fracture can happen when a bone is stressed repeatedly or overused in an unhealthy way. Though it's often used to describe things physically, it has become the metaphor for what happens to me (and others) emotionally. Through life-events, trauma, or even chemical imbalance, our soul can undergo repetitive stress that eventually forms an internal stress fracture of sorts. Thus, we can say of ourselves we have a "stress-fracture of the soul," as an attempt to give words to a state of being which we lack adequate descriptors.

This brings up another question. What do I mean by using the term "soul"? Let me explain it this way: We as human beings are body, spirit, and soul. Each term describes a completely different portion of what makes up who we are as a human being.

- Body - Our physical selves.
- Soul - Our mind, will, and emotions.
- Spirit - The innermost and eternal part of us.

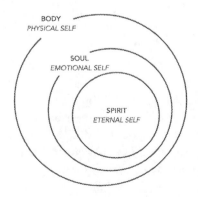

The body is the easiest to understand as most of us understands this part of us that tangibly connects to the physical world with our five senses (touch, taste, sight, hearing, and smell). The other two can be a bit more difficult to grasp as I know people who struggle with separating the concept of soul versus spirit.

Maybe I can describe it this way:

The spirit is eternal, the part of us that manifests faith.

The soul is the internal part of us that manifests emotions and personality.

Why is this so important to understand? Each of the three parts heavily influences the other. For example, if you have a physical injury (body) that prevents you from having what you might consider a "normal" life, you may be apt to feel discouraged (soul), or even go into some depression (soul) that may affect your view on God (spirit) and endurance (body).

We can even go in the other direction. Say you put your faith in Christ (spirit). That decision in your innermost being connects to how you feel about your life (soul) and how you live in the physical world (body). What I'm trying to illustrate is that these three parts of us are interconnected. What happens in one area can and will have an impact in the others. Why make that connection? It's because it helps us to recognize that the health of our soul is directly connected to the health of our body and our spirit. It also reminds us that when one area is injured, it can drastically affect the other parts.

What I hope our society can begin to recognize is that depression is an injury. Our souls are hurting. We may not know what caused it nor what continues to feed it, but one thing we do know: our soul is fractured and we are in pain. Even worse, we don't always know what to do about it or how to fix it.

It hurts here

There's an old joke from my childhood about a person who went to the doctor because everything on their body hurt to the touch. The doctor listened to the patient and said, "*Point to all of the parts of your body that are painful.*" So the patient touched his knee and said, "*Ouch.*" He then proceeded to touch other parts of his body. From his shoulder to his neck, to his elbow, to his foot, everything he touched, he responded with, "*Ouch.*"

"*Doctor, do you know what's wrong?*"

"*Yes. You have a broken finger.*"

Terrible joke? Yep (even though I am currently laughing at it while I write this). The point of the joke is to be taken in the context of depression. To us, our whole world hurts because everything within that world is *touched* by our darkness. Our bodies feel drained. Our soul is weary. Our spirits are starving for faith.

Somewhere, somehow, an injury has taken place and it's created an open emotional laceration. Left untreated, this internal wound becomes a portal for the darkness to attack and take over.

My wounds have traditionally happened in a variety of ways:

- Rejection from people
- Unmet expectations
- A chemical unbalance
- Disappointment
- Comparing myself to others
- A let down from a trusted source
- Failure (on my part or others)

Take your pick.

What we must see is how important it is to realize that an injury to our soul affects everything about us. Our soul is that connection point between what is the innermost part of us and our physical expression to the rest of the world. It's here where unexpected injuries can happen. Some may call it "emotional strain" or "emotional hurts." Again, I prefer to use the terminology of having a stress-fracture in my soul. Something caused some repetitive stress inside of me that has created trauma that an MRI or X-ray cannot detect. A lot of the hurts are deep within the abyss of our memories and our feelings embedded so far within us that it may even be hidden from ourselves.

For many of us, we don't even know how to articulate what is "wrong" and/or what is ailing inside of us. We just know something is hurt. Something within us is ailing and, during our shadow-moments, we are going through the torture of our emotions self-navigating us all over the place. My feelings urge me to keep selecting random mentalities that keep me from understanding what I'm going through versus what I'm supposed to feel.

In the middle of it all lies a well-meaning human *trying* to help.

"What's wrong? Use your words"

If I've heard it once, I've heard it a thousand times, "*Just tell me what's wrong.*" I wish it was that easy. Ask a counselor sometime how long it takes someone who's dealing with depression to try to articulate both what's wrong and what they think we need. Let's be real, we want the lives we perceive everybody else possesses that somehow escapes us. Those of us navigating depression assume everyone is having the best day and/or life, except for us. Those we love who are watching us tend to say things like:

Can't you just snap out of it? No.

Just cheer up. Sounds great. I wish that was an option.

Fake it till you make it. So, you just want me to put up a front because I'm making YOU uncomfortable.

Stop being sad. Great. I feel "fixed" now.

You're a Christian. Guilt. What a great motivator.

Choose joy. Okay. I'll get back to you when I feel that's within the realm of possibility for me.

It's ignorant statements like these that make us either bury our pain a bit deeper and/or mask it better. We are already uncomfortable internally. We hate the way we feel. It's when we see that our depression is being noticed and it's affecting others, we'll either distance ourselves or we will work harder to conceal our struggles. That may seem like a lot of work to you who've never gone through depression, but we are used to it.

You see, those of us who live in the shadows have become accustomed to looking the part. Personally, I know how to smile at church. I can get myself to work and listen to others. I can put on my "professional camouflage" and blend in. However, inside something is "off"; something feels broken. It's like this: You know in your head what you want to do but your body and your emotions are acting as if they are in complete control.

"But Dave, don't you want to stop feeling that way?"

Of course, I don't want to feel this way. Any of us who deal with the shadows would love to never have to face depression. But when you are in the thick of it, all you know in that moment is, regardless of how good life can be or even appear, my emotions are "self-navigating" all over the place. And when I try to select a new emotion or a new thought, my feelings take over and want to "navigate" me in another direction. Rational thought isn't always there. If you've never dealt with depression, then you don't know that your rational wisdom that sounds so simple may feel extremely complex to someone who's currently under the thumb of their inner darkness. You may have your emotions in full control 100% of the time, 365 days a year (or at least you try to appear that way). For us, we must periodically have a wrestling match over who's in control of our lives. Will we allow truth to guide us? Or will we allow our feelings to self-navigate our lives into chaos?

This is our battle. This is our plight. And what we need is not someone trying to "fix us." We just need someone there for us.

Who's fault?

There's a story in Scripture that has always caught my eye, not because of the circumstance but because of those who were watching the situation take place. In the ninth chapter of John, it starts off,

"As Jesus was walking along, he saw a man who had been blind from birth."

(John 9:1 NLT)

Look at those words. He was born with a condition. The man didn't ask for this nor did he do anything to deserve it. He was born this way.

Then the next verse hits hard.

"Rabbi," his disciples asked him, "why was this man born blind?

51

Was it because of his own sins or his parents' sins?"

(John 9:2 NLT)

A couple thoughts go through my mind.

My first thought is wrapped around the reason why you have to be careful when you go through suffering. In the presence of pain, we can be so quick to jump to all sorts of assumptions as to *"what did I do to invite this?"* There is a trick of Satan, a lie which leads you to believe that ANY suffering or darkness you go through is a direct result of something that you caused. I've sat up many long nights pondering what I did to deserve the seasons of darkness. I've wasted too many moments pondering about how I caused this to happen to me. Those momentary thoughts turned into days, if not weeks, of self-induced anguish as I tried to work through what I did to cause these dark feelings. Many in generations before ours have considered this type of behavior as self-indulgence or mere emotional immaturity, furthering the whispers in our ears to stay isolated while we get ourselves sorted, so as to not bring others down with our anguish.

Let me say this loud and clear so those in the back row can hear:

Suffering is not always the result of personal sin!

Let's be real, there are times where we live out the consequences of sins we committed. I won't gloss over that. Sin bears a heavy toll on our cumulative self - that is, spirit, soul, and body. It attacks us from the inside out. I'm thankful for the forgiveness of God which pardons us of the eternal effects of our sin. That said, many times we still experience the earthly ramifications of what our sin had set into motion.

Yet there is internal suffering that people go through every day that cannot be attributed to any sin. There's been no direct correlation to any misdeed or misconduct. There is a condition that has caused suffering that has no rhyme or reason. There is just the presence of pain.

The second thought was the response of Jesus' disciples. Instead of being fully present with this man, they looked for the reason behind his condition. Were they showing off for their Rabbi (teacher)? Were the Disciples trying to flex their spiritual intuition by trying to diagnose the situation?

"*We've got this figured out. Either he messed up or his parents did.*" In that day, there was a superstition that if there was a condition that wasn't healthy, the only explanation was the direct result of sin.

"*Somebody caused this so we must find someone to blame.*" Their response really doesn't surprise me. It was a very cultural reaction.

"*Somebody has to be to blame. Why? Anyone God loves wouldn't have to deal with this problem.*" There was an assumption that problems equated to God pulling away from you.

They were so bent on figuring out the "why" that they forgot about the "who." These followers of Jesus were so busy flexing their spiritual insight they failed to understand that there was a human being behind the condition that needed someone to be fully present with him.

One of the areas where depression wants to rob human beings is that our condition swallows up the "who." We lose our identities to the point where we can only see the condition. We are blinding to the possibilities of life because darkness shrouds everything around us.

We're too broken to have friendships like everyone else.

We're too broken to be qualified for the same job as someone else.

We're too broken to have a happy marriage.

We're too broken to be quality parents.

We're so broken that God won't waste His time on us.

All of this is compounded when the people closest see us struggling and, instead of treating us as a human, attempt to label us as a condition, try to fix us, or perhaps worse, keep their distance from us. I'm very glad that when I read the Scriptures, I see a Jesus who chooses to see something in us.

The blame game doesn't work

I love how Jesus replied to this whole situation.

"It was not because of his sins or his parents' sins," Jesus answered.

"This happened so the power of God could be seen in him."

(John 9:3 NLT)

Jesus grabs their attention to simply say: Look deeper. There's no sin. There's nothing to "figure out" in terms of who's fault this is. There's only a person standing here wondering if anyone, including God, cares about them. This man needs more than a token comment. He needs genuine compassion.

After all, the Scripture says he was *"blind from birth."* This is something that he's always known about. Living in darkness is second nature. It's nothing new to him. Assigning blame doesn't fix anything, it just gives a new direction for anger, hate, and resentment. My guess is that this is all this man knew for most of his life of living in darkness.

In our blame-driven culture, it seems we are always looking for someone or something to blame. If something is wrong, I blame a politician for what he/she is allowing. If I see something in my life I don't like, I blame my parents for how they raised me. If I am in debt, I blame the economy. Blame is our drug of choice and the payoff is that blame defers responsibility to somebody else. Better said, blame gives us the excuse for inactivity.

When Jesus' companions are looking for the cause, what they're really saying is, *"Who's at fault so that those people can take care of this situation?"* Jesus halted that mentality! He wanted to shift their view of this man from a casualty of someone else's faults to a candidate for a Miracle of God. Even typing that causes me to breathe a sigh of relief. When I'm in my darkest place, I don't need someone to blame (I already do enough of that and usually I'm blaming myself). I need someone that can see what I cannot see. I need people who can do more than diagnose my condition but step into it and give authentic hope.

For those of you reading that have never dealt with depression, let me tell you that hope seems possible for everyone except those of us in the shadows. It's a mentality that we can't simply turn on and off.

"Stop thinking that way."

Can you imagine saying that to this blind man? *"Excuse me sir, stop being blind."* As silly as that sounds, people say that to those of us who deal with depression as if we can turn it on and off with an act of our will. If we could, we would. I'm convinced that the more we understand mental and emotional sickness, the more we'd empathize with the struggles of others in our lives.

What can you do? Do what Jesus did. Give us hope.

Give me a glass of water

When I think of what hope is like to people dealing with depression, the first image to comes to mind is this:

A glass of water.

So simple. So clean. Yet in a world where we have a plethora of beverage choices, we take for granted what flows out of our faucets.

Water is essential to this planet that it is vital to all known forms of life. In fact, we wouldn't be here without it. It provides neither food nor energy. Nutrients and oxygen are carried by water to all the cells of our body. It regulates our body temperature. Water stabilizes our heartbeat. It protects our organs and tissues, it maximizes our physical performance, and promotes healthy brain function.

Why is hope like a glass of water?

Because hope, like water, is essential for human life. It keeps us moving forward day to day (and on some days, hour to hour). It provides neither money for your bills nor puts food on your tables. Yet it carries expectation to every part of our lives. Hope stabilizes our hearts to believe for better days. It protects our soul, helps us to function emotionally, and promotes healthy thinking.

So yes, hope is like a glass of water. It is exactly what we need in our darkest moments. Hope. We don't need your understanding as much as we need a sense of anticipation and expectation that things will be better. Hope. We don't need your solution as much as we need the presence of a friend who won't leave us broken and alone. Hope. Unless you're a licensed counselor, we don't need your solutions and prescriptions of what we *should* do as much as we need a listening ear that doesn't default to judgment. Hope. We are emotionally blind and crying out for help. Hope. People have been tossing us their token comments but that hasn't worked. Hope. Please, just hope.

Give us hope.

Survival Tips for the Shadows:
Authentic Friendships Need Healthy Boundaries

A target is something we aim at with the goal of hitting the middle (the "*bullseye*"). The center is then surrounded by concentric circles that grow larger.

This is the metaphor I use to help people develop necessary boundaries with friendships. Boundaries are needed because not everyone in your life should have equal access and equal influence. Not everyone's words and actions should possess the same weight. This is achieved by creating intentional, healthy boundaries.

Boundaries are best created out of love for yourself and others. When properly executed, boundaries can help establish how the friendships and connections function in your life and how close certain people *should* be based on *your* overall health. Of course you love all of your friends deeply, but you should navigate each of your relationships separately, in both trust and availability.

You'll have "*bullseye*" people. Your inner circle. These are people you can say anything to any time, anywhere. They are Christ-centered, confidential, and have your best interest in mind (I keep about 3 people there). As you move out from the center, you will have additional layers of trust and closeness. Place your relationships on those other layers. The closer to the "*bullseye*," the more influential and dependable they are. The further out on the board, you won't treat them as lesser or inferior, but you will know that this group won't have as much access to nor information from you. It may be because they can't handle confidential information. Perhaps they have broken trust. Maybe you think they have a tendency to "gossip."

NOTE: We don't just cut off friends and turn the page. We move them out from the center. If they become toxic, that's when they get moved "off the board" so to speak.

Through different seasons of life, I will move some friendships further out and some friendships closer to the "*bullseye*." That depends upon my emotional state, my personal needs, my personal growth, as well as the growth of others.

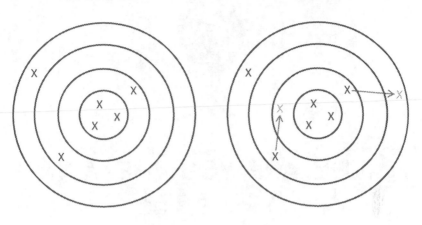

SEASON ONE   SEASON TWO

Take some time to draw out a target and ask yourself where the people in your life fall on the board and what boundaries you should have. Remember, this is done out of love for yourself and others. It is easy to assign boundaries reactively when done out of anger, spite, or any other emotion. It is also common to want to allow anyone who is "interested" into your inner circle based upon their personality or relationship to you. Be warned, if they don't have personal integrity, your best interest at heart, or have good boundaries themselves, they may not be the best "*bullseye*" people. For example, perhaps they like to share a little too much of other peoples' business, or their life is not an example to strive for, then they should not be in the center of your circle. Take care in the amount of time you give them and the amount of your heart that you share with them. Remember, this is about the boundaries your mental health needs. Assign the boundaries out of love for yourself and others, and ask God for help if it is not clear where to start.

- 4 -

WHY ARE YOU THE WAY YOU ARE?

I've been strong and I've been broken within a moment
I've been faithful and I've been reckless at every bend
I've held everything together and watched it shatter
I've stood tall and I have crumbled in the same breath
I was found before I was lost
I was Yours before I was not
Grace to spare for all my mistakes
And that part just wrecks me

"As You Find Me" by Hillsong United

"A fool lets it all hang out; a sage quietly mulls it over."
Proverbs 29:11 MSG

I can't say that I'm the most talented person in the world, but I do have a very particular set of skills that I've acquired over a very long career. These "skills" have been recognized over and over, not only by my wife, but also those in my inner circle. The skill I am the most proud of is my ability to memorize quotes from movies and TV shows after seeing them only once (hence the lines I just used from the movie *Taken*).

Before anyone judges me, many of you likely do the same thing. You grab quotes from your favorite film or television series and sprinkle them in random moments and conversations. Why do we do that? Who knows. There is just something so satisfying about using the proper on-screen excerpt for the right real-life situation.

For example, I love the show "*The Office*." This iconic piece of television history has a plethora of famous quotes and moments. One of my favorites is when the character Michael Scott decides to verbalize to his coworker Toby how much he despises him. He starts off by asking the question:

"*Why are you the way you are?*"

I remember how funny I thought the scene was when I initially watched it. Not only did it lead to a hilarious rant, but I've found it as my comedic "go-to" for moments at home or in my workday to highlight how different the personalities are between me, my staff, and even my family.

"*Why are you the way you are?*"

As time has gone by, this piece of TV humor has become more than a funny tagline but an all too real question I ultimately ask of myself. When the shadows of depression linger over me, an internal monologue begins inside of my head. And the "go-to" line is always the same:

"David, why are you the way you are?"

When I'm going through the "*shadows*," I tend to get angry or frustrated at myself for feeling the way that I do. I tell myself, "*David, you have no right to be THIS sad.*" Like many people, we start off with a reactionary approach instead of an introspective one. We attack others well before we take inventory both in our relationships and within ourselves.

The self-talk ensues as the self-defeating thoughts begin to flow:

How can I justify being this down when others have it worse than me?

What is so wrong with me that I cannot get it together like everyone else can?

Should I steal a counselor's time when they could be helping someone else?

Stop your crying and grow up.

You are an embarrassment and a fraud.

Then that anger turns to self-loathing as I begin to assign blame to myself.

What have I done to deserve this?

This depression is obviously my fault.

If I'd been a better person, there's no way I would go through this.

I've obviously done something to cause this to happen.

There are those reading this who know exactly what I'm talking about. You've sat in moments of sadness that were dripping with hopelessness wondering what you specifically did to cause this. What may be a simple chemical unbalance in your body or unhealed trauma in your life translates into self-contempt. What could be living in the effects of a pain in your past only registers as, "you, and you alone, are at fault." Many times, the only conclusion I can comprehend of myself is this: if one thing is broken internally, then I must be completely broken as a human. Thus, life becomes prey to the predatory approach of the misuse of "self-talk."

"It's just a scratch"

Everyone engages in something called *"self-talk."* I'd define self-talk as the internal dialogue we use as the framework for which we navigate the circumstances we find ourselves in. Used properly, it can be an instrument of personal challenge and encouragement, an effective tool of inspiration and motivation. In the scriptures, it was said that King David *"encouraged himself in the Lord"* (1 Samuel 30:6 KJV). His self-talk was like an internal coach pushing him forward. Like any tool, what could be used to edify (to build up), can also be weaponized to tear down others or ourselves. The internal dialogue we exercise should be used to encourage or build up? If your mind isn't in the right place, it can easily be harnessed to tear yourself and others apart.

When I think of self-talk, I think of music. As a Gen-Xer, I can say I've grown through a vast array of musical genres listening to my favorite artists. I've lived through 8-tracks, cassettes, CDs, and mp3s. If I had to pick a favorite, I'd still choose listening to music on vinyl. For me, there is something so simple and pure about the way music is played in this historic fashion which I find very comforting.

As a collector of vinyl records, the one thing I don't want is a deep scratch on them. This seemingly small blemish can happen through mishandling the disc, not properly caring for it, or by some accidental event.

The problem with a scratch is if the turntable needle finds it, the needle can get stuck in that spot playing the same part of the song over and over; unable to move ahead to the next track. Often, when there's a scratch, you begin to stay away from that album altogether. You'd rather listen to something else than deal with a track skipping because of a scratch.

This is such an accurate description of what happens within the self-talk or internal dialogue of those of us who deal with depression. A moment happens, sometimes through no malicious or intentional event, and an injury appears in the fabric of our soul (we'll just call it a "*scratch*"). Much like a vinyl record, that moment will get played over and over in our minds as we fixate on what's been hurt rather than seeing the whole picture.

Our internal dialogue will begin to say things like:

- "*Why can't anything good happen to me?*"
- "*You will never get beyond this.*"
- "*Everyone looks so 'normal'; why am I the only one who is hurting?*"
- "*Why am I the only one going through this?*"
- "*I'll never change.*"

Through unhealthy internal dialogue, we've taken a "*scratch*" and we've turned it into a "*system.*" Instead of recognizing that we've visited a moment of hurt, we've made it the address to live at and form our lives around. When unhealthy self-talk is part of your life, it is so challenging to move past it and it can feel impossible to think outside of it. Why? First, it's difficult to move beyond what you may be allowing to replay over and over in your mind. Some traumatic events can continuously rerun in our thoughts all on their own. I'm not talking about that. I am referring to the purposeful fixation on moments, not to learn from them, but rather allow yourself to dwell on them and relive them.

Second, when images in your mind turn to words in your heart, it may feel like it solidifies an identity in your life. We all must understand that every statement you tell yourself matters. I like how the Scriptures describe this in Proverbs 23:7 (NASB), "*For as he thinks within himself, so he is.*" So, we take moments that have happened and instead of learning from them, we see a world that is unattainable based upon what we tell ourselves about our hurts.

My friends, believe me, there is a better way to live!

"Use your inside voice"

Tattooed on my right wrist is "Psalm 42:5." I see it every day when I type or reach for my phone. It has become the scripture I lean into daily as well as every time I feel the shadow creeping into my soul. In fact, the entire Psalm (including chapter 43) is the passage that I preach from whenever I'm invited to speak about my journey through depression. My hope is that this book will be to others what Psalm 42-43 has meant to me: a means by which I can see that someone, besides me, deals with turmoil in my soul. Not only that, but the author of Psalm 42 practices self-talk.

Psalm 42 is a song of lament written by someone who formerly was able to freely worship God with others. However, something has happened; the circumstances changed. As you read the Psalm, the author begins to articulate the deep sadness in his soul. He feels removed, even isolated, from the time of life that he formerly enjoyed. He looks at the past with pain longingly wishing he could return to better times.

As you read his words, you come across what seems to not be a prayer to God but some interior dialogue.

"Why am I discouraged? Why is my heart so sad? I will put my hope in God! I will praise him again—my Savior and my God!"

(Psalm 42:5-6 NLT)

This Psalmist is exercising healthy "self-talk."

Many commentators of Scripture believe that both Psalms 42 and 43 are one song that was split into two. If that's the case, this author repeats these words of self-talk three times. A general rule of bible reading says that when something is repeated three times, it means that point or detail is meant to be emphasized.

Perhaps the emphasis is on the fact that he's in a personal struggle. I can see that, and quite frankly, it encourages me that I'm not alone. Maybe the author is wanting others to be encouraged that Godly people have days and moments like this. I catch that and appreciate normalizing these challenging seasons. Too often, Christians can misdiagnose these seasons as moments connected to a lack of faith or the presence of sin. Neither come into play to encounter the shadows.

As valid as those points are, I feel this specific wording and the repetition of the statements point more to an emphasis not for our sake, per se, but for his. He's emphasizing to himself, over and over, that there is life beyond his personal darkness. He calls out truth in the midst of his feelings. The despair is so deep that he needs to underscore to himself that his feelings, though valid and important, are necessary to be acknowledged, but cannot lead our lives. Better said, feelings can be great advisors, but they make terrible bosses.

Truth must, must, must (three times for emphasis) be what leads us. It has to be what guides us through the shadows despite what our emotions may be speaking. Jesus said of himself,

> *"I am the way, the truth, and the life. No one can come to the Father except through me."*

> (John 14:6 NLT)

This Psalmist uses self-talk to stress to himself the fact that, yes, life at the moment is a struggle, BUT better days are coming. If God has been faithful in the past, He WILL be faithful again. Presently life is challenging. Much like a Michigan winter, this status seems like it's not going away, but Spring is coming. Better days are ahead.

When I talk about self-talk, I'm not talking about being "positive" for positive's sake. This is not "mind over matter." I can hear some people say, "Self-talk is just positive thinking," as if thinking positive was harmful or systemic of being passive about your problems. Positive self-talk is good, but what we really need is *truthful* self-talk. In other words, finding something positive to ponder upon is good and can have some benefits, but what positions you to burst out of the shadows is that which needs to trump our feelings: Truth.

Truthful self-talk is what we need to help us through the shadows. Positive self-talk may get us motivated to move forward, but truthful self-talk is what helps us to power through. Why? Again, truth trumps feelings. I love the Scripture in John 8:32 NLT:

> *"and you shall KNOW the truth and the truth shall set you free."*
> (emphasis mine)

The key word is *"know."* The truth is central to your thinking and it's what guides you in and through your shadows into freedom.

Obviously, this list is not at all exhaustive. I could fill up this chapter with statements both you and I have made during dark moments. Personally, I have specific Scriptures that I lean into during my shadow times to help guide me in Truth whenever I can't see or sense it. I have learned to do the preparatory work of finding the

EMOTIONAL "REALITY"	TRUTHFUL SELF-TALK
"I feel abandoned."	"God will never leave me or forsake me." *(Hebrews 13:5 NLT)*
"I feel lost."	"God will always guide me." *(Isaiah 58:11 NLT)*
"I feel hurt and alone."	"When I'm hurting, God draws close to me." *(Psalm 34:18 NLT)*
"I feel overwhelmed."	"God is my strength, comfort, and place of safety." *(Psalm 61:1-3 NLT)*

"rescue" Scriptures during the emotionally healthy days, instead of waiting to look for them when life feels like a struggle. It's like waiting to check the batteries in your flashlight until you lose power. At the end of this chapter, I'm including a page for you to write out the statements you speak to yourself during your shadowy times, and the corresponding truthful self-talk you will need in those moments. Pray over that list. If you need help, seek out some wise, Godly counsel.

"You win or lose on one square foot of real estate"

Let's admit: We need truthful speaking. It's important and prophetic. It's not about "*naming it and claiming it*" such as in the context of the prosperity movement of Christianity where you can "claim" anything you want in Jesus' name and think God is going to automatically give it to you. It's about being willing to speak that which you know is true even if you don't see it. There's validity to speaking out by faith what God may do next in your life.

Truthful self-talk is a fantastic tool. However, what we can't do with it is to relegate it to only what comes out of our mouths but what is allowing our minds. Better said, truthful self-talk includes, not just what comes out of our mouths but also healthy thinking. I've met people who will confess the right words with their mouths yet are unwilling to change their thinking. You need both.

If we all possess self-talk (and I believe we do), then there needs to be a consistent, healthy atmosphere inside our minds. Our thinking is the place where all our internal dialogue takes place. It's also the battlefield where wars are won and lost.

When I was growing up, to emphasize healthy thinking, I'd hear preachers talk about how battles are won and lost on one square foot of real estate: our minds. Though the measurements may not be completely accurate, I think there's some truth to this metaphor.

I remember my freshman year of football facing a team that had the same record as us. It was the last game of the year, and we wanted a statement game for two reasons. First, it was the final game and you want to end on a winning note. Second, we were going to merge with this team the following year in the local high school. We were warming up and the atmosphere was fun yet focused, until we saw the other team get off the bus. I remember feeling the tone of our pre-game change. Something shifted.

In that moment, we had transformed from excitement and anticipation to,

"Look how huge they are!"

"We can't block them."

"How are we going to stop them?"

"They can't be the same age as us."

I remember it like it was yesterday. In one moment, we had abandoned all confidence and lost the game well before it had started. Before we lost on the football fields, we lost on "one square foot of real estate." We lost the game in our minds before the game even started.

It reminds me of perhaps the most famous stories of Scripture. 1 Samuel 17 tells us the story of David and Goliath. When we think about the story, we ponder a young boy who came and took down a giant. A closer examination would help us see that this is a story in which an entire army was losing a battle, simply because of negative self-talk.

The Scripture tells us that when a giant named Goliath came out from the opposing army, Israel's army was *"terrified and deeply shaken"* (1 Samuel 17:11 NLT). It goes on to say, *"As soon as the Israelite army saw him, they began to run away in fright. 'Have you seen the giant?' the men asked. He comes out each day to defy Israel."* (1 Samuel 17:124-25a NLT). If this was their *external* dialogue, you can imagine their *internal* self-talk. They hadn't picked up a sword or a spear to battle with, yet they had already lost the fight on one square foot of real estate.

This army of Israel was well trained for battle. They were prepared and experienced. This was not a batch of young recruits. Yet what was happening in the present moment so consumed their thinking that it shook them from not just *who* they were but *whose* they were. They forgot God was on their side!

God had brought them out of slavery and into a new land, God had established them as a people and a nation. The people asked for a king, and He provided. This was the army of the Living God. Israel was God's chosen people. However, the presence of a single man (though a very big man) crushed their spirits and paralyzed them in fear.

Isn't that what our depression does? It takes a moment and tries to eclipse the light in our lives. It takes a present situation and tries to give us such tunnel vision that all we can see or detect is the struggle and not the solution. As we become fixated on the darkness, we lose the plot of the greater narrative at hand. Proverbs 23:7 KJV says it best, *"For as a man thinks in his heart so he is..."*. That simply means that what we place as central in our mentality becomes our primary focus and we begin to live that out. Simply said, bad thinking creates toxic self-talk. Toxic self-talk leads to moments like what we see here. We are frozen in the moment, unable to move forward. Trapped in the shadows.

Enter David.

I know who I am.

This small shepherd boy comes on the scene completely innocent. His only task is to deliver a care package to his brothers. Like any young sibling, he wants to hang around to see what his brothers and their friends are up to, or better said, up against. Quickly, David becomes privy to the situation at hand and begins to ask about the prize for standing up to the giant. In 1 Samuel 17, you'll see he doesn't ask about the size of the obstacle but rather the reward for overcoming it. David's mindset is one of victory, not defeat. He knew of a simple truth: God is faithful. God helped him in the past with seemingly impossible situations. Why wouldn't He do it again?

Almost immediately, David is met with verbal hostility by his brothers. They attack his role in life, his motives for being there, and his qualifications for giving input. When I had previously read this part of the Scripture, I used to get frustrated with David's siblings, however, if I slip inside of their skin, I can completely understand (but not excuse) their reactions. They've been beaten down emotionally and mentally for days by a giant. Most likely, they've been beating themselves up for not stepping up and doing something about Goliath. They were frozen by fear, and having a young, untrained, non-soldier step up with boldness had to be embarrassing. That's what depression does to us. It wants to hold us under its thumb stifling us of any activity or any possibility of hope. In our heads, we *ought* to be able to move forward, but because we *feel* we can't, we end up beating ourselves up, thus losing the battle of our minds. We lose the conflict over our intellect, reasoning, and our imagination.

David is so good here. His internal dialogue isn't about comparing himself to what he is facing, but comparing what he is facing to who God is. I love his words, *"Who is this pagan Philistine anyway, that he is allowed to defy the armies of the Living God?"* (1 Samuel 17:26 NLT). Unlike the armies of Israel, David knew *who* he was (a servant of God) and *whose* he was (he belonged *to* God). He spoke out in confidence what he knew to be true, even if it was controversial to the people he was surrounded with.

In her book, *Switch On Your Brain*, Dr. Caroline Leaf says, *"As we think, we change the physical nature of our brain. As we consciously direct our thinking, we can wire out toxic patterns of thinking and replace them with healthy thoughts."* David could have accepted the toxic patterns of his brothers (and everyone else's for that matter) into his own thinking. Instead, David chose to direct his thinking to that which he knew to be true: God has never failed him. And what God did before, He can do again.

The reason why I spend so much time on this portion of this chapter is because those of us who walk through the shadows stare at giants all the time. Far too often, we lose the battle on our own *"one square foot of real estate."* We get why the soldiers were paralyzed mentally and emotionally. We get why they were embarrassed seeing someone else step up when internally we are telling ourselves, *"That should be you. Why can't you step up? What is wrong with you?"* We all want to be a "David" but end up like one of his brothers. That's where this story leads us to hope.

Even as David steps up, the battle of his mentality isn't finished yet. He faces a giant, clad in armor and weaponry, with a staff, a sling, and a few rocks. Goliath begins to hurl insults at him trying to demean him back into the shadows where the entire Israelite army is residing. Goliath says, *"Am I a dog...that you come at me with a stick?"* (1 Samuel 17:43 NLT) I believe David's attention would have been drawn to the staff he carried. You see, a shepherd, like David, carried his staff every day and everywhere. When anything monumental or meaningful happened, a shepherd would have carved that memory into his staff. That staff was covered in stories of God's faithfulness to David.

So, when the mocking voice came at him about carrying a stick, instead of triggering more fear, it triggered faith. Why? David's eyes would have been locked onto that staff and the etchings on it. Every mark, every scribble, would have reminded him of every monumental victory God had provided. Talk about a backfire on Goliath. He meant to get into David's head; he didn't anticipate igniting faith in David's heart.

Victory is contagious

It shouldn't surprise us that David responded with not just courageousness, but also with confidence in taking out a simple stone, placing it in his sling, and knocking down the giant that emotionally paralyzed everyone else. When Goliath's body hit the ground, the interior dialogue of every single man in Israel's army changed. Why? Victory is contagious. When you get it, everyone wants in.

Maybe you're reading this today struggling with your thinking. Perhaps your thought processes and emotions have left you feeling defeated even before the battle has begun. Can you take a cue from David? In the face of the opposition you may feel, can you focus on truth?

Let me help you with some truth to focus on:

You are loved by God, whether you can hear him right now or not.

You are loved by others, whether you believe it or not.

You possess value, whether you can feel it or not.

You have purpose here in this life, whether you can sense it or not.

You are a gift to this world, whether you realize it or not.

These statements are TRUTH. Nothing you can do (or feel) can separate you from God's love. *He finds so much value in you that He sent His Son to lay down His life for you!* You are here because God has a purpose for your life. You are distinctly and uniquely gifted and blessed, not because of some deed(s) you have performed to earn it, but simply because you are a child of God.

Listen, I understand the battlefield of our minds and the internal dialogue it produces. I'll admit, many times my "inside voice" is PG-13 or worse. It can get rough, but then again, that's what happens in battle. Always remember, your mind is worth the fight. God has given you truth, to fight that battle, and to win the war.

There's a saying I got from a friend who is a personal trainer. "*You can't outwork bad eating habits.*" So, no matter how much you run or workout, if the diet you consume isn't as healthy as the effort you are giving, then you are defeating yourself and the goals you have set. Your mind lives off what you feed it. Truthful self-talk flows out of intentional healthy thinking habits. What we saw in the army of Israel was people who did the work of being soldiers. They had the equipment and the ability. Because they mentally fed their minds fear and anxiety, they were stuck, unable to move forward. These men of warfare were paralyzed as a result of what they were fueling their minds.

Feed your mind faith and truth. The Apostle Paul would say it this way,

Fix your thoughts on what is true, and honorable, and right, and pure, and lovely, and admirable. Think about things that are excellent and worthy of praise.

Philippians 4:8 NLT

That word *"fix"* is used strategically. It's a purposeful action; an intentional decision. Paul is saying that you need to willingly decide to feed your mind that which will build your faith by consuming what is true. Do you feel paralyzed by your emotions? Start feeding your mind on faith and truth. Open up the Scriptures with a trusted friend. Lean into a healthy faith community. Have a conversation with a Christ-centered clinician. Spend time in prayer by yourself. Entrust your challenges with those in your life who are gifted in prayer. Journal out your thoughts. Listen to music that will feed your soul. Quiet yourself to hear God's direction.

As you consume what is healthy, don't be surprised when you begin to recognize habits and thought processes that don't belong. You'll begin to see the toxic mindsets (and their sources) that have been leaching joy from your life. You will begin to make healthier choices that will lead to an abundant and healthier life. This was David. He was willing to feed his mind what was true of God and what was true of himself. That enabled him to see Goliath for what he really was. To the soldiers stuck in their anxiety, the giant was a roadblock to defeat. To David, because of what he fed his mind, Goliath became an opportunity for victory.

Friends, there will always be giants to face. Sometimes you face them in the physical sense. It could be a difficult relationship, a task to perform at work, or a challenging situation you have to face. These are often easy to see though they're not easy to handle. If I'm really honest, the giants that I struggle with the most are not the one's I see but the one's deep inside of me. They are the interior battles that cannot be ignored. The giants must be faced; they must be confronted.

Whether you feel like it or not, I see you as a "David." You are a giant-defeating warrior. What it's going to take today is to feed your mind well and to take a stand against what desires to rule your mind.

They say, "You are what you eat." Today, feed on faith and truth. When you do, don't be surprised to see a boldness rise as you begin to step forward, boldly taking down the giants in your path.

Survival Tips for the Shadows:
Truthful Self-Talk

Below (or in your journal), take some time to write out the negative statements that you are prone to telling yourself in times of doubt or darkness. Across from that statement, I'd like you to challenge yourself to write a new, Christ-centered statement of positive, truthful self-talk. The next time your mind wants to feed you what isn't true, step forward with what you know to be true of God and yourself.

"NEGATIVE STATEMENT"	"TRUTHFUL STATEMENT"
Example: "I am unnoticed and lonely."	"I am loved and cared for by God."

- 5 -

TRIGGER HAPPY

I know the night won't last
Your Word will come to pass
My heart will sing Your praise again
Your promise still stands
Great is Your faithfulness, faithfulness
I'm still in Your hands
This is my confidence, You never failed

"Do it Again" by Elevation Worship

"A fool lets it all hang out; a sage quietly mulls it over."
Proverbs 29:11 MSG

Where would we be without YouTube? Remember the days of trying to find an actual in-person human being who has a specific skill or expertise to ask questions about something you need to fix? You "YouTube it." Home project? YouTube it. Want to do crafts? YouTube it. Need a workout? YouTube it. Need surgery? Please don't YouTube that. Go see a medical professional.

Our family has embraced this. Often, if my wife gives me a task on the "honey do" list, I may say, *"I'm not sure how to do this."* Her response is always the same: "Just YouTube it." For example, almost everyone in my family has taken off a mirror on the car backing out of the garage. Never once have I ever fixed a mirror on a car out of my own knowledge, let alone, on three different cars. How did I fix them? YouTube.

You can find a cornucopia of content on the site. Some of it is entertaining. As stated, some of it is helpful. Some of it is…well… interesting. My advice to people with YouTube (and anything on the internet) is to use wisdom and discernment. Use sound thinking and Spirit-led understanding. It will help you sort through the muck and mire. One of my favorite quotes that I've seen online says it best:

"Not everything you read on the internet is true."

- Abraham Lincoln

On YouTube, there is a feature that helps you see the videos that are "trending." What that means is there are videos that are appealing to a large number of viewers and YouTube highlights them because it thinks you might be interested. One of them caught my eye. They are called ASMR videos. I'd soon find out that it's one of the most popular types of videos out there (at least at the time this book was being written). According to thinkwithgoogle.com, this type of video has become a cultural phenomenon. What started off as a few videos posted in 2013 has grown into million videos some of which have millions of views per video. ASMR videos are not a "15-minutes of fame" type of trend. This one is sticking.

If you are not familiar with the acronym, it means "Autonomic Sensory Meridian Response." The videos play sound along with visual cues that are intended to generate what's described as a type of "tingling" sensation in the viewer. The sensation starts in the scalp, then travels down the neck and into the spine. Some say it's like the sensation of goosebumps, but inside your body. Others will talk about how listening or watching them will bring a sense of calm. To name a few, "Sound Cues" include typing, whispering, clicking, tapping, or scratching. "Visual cues" include things like people mixing paint, brushing hair, or even slicing soft objects.

There isn't a ton of research on this phenomenon, but empirical data shows thousands of people are using ASMR videos all over the world to calm themselves and/or to help them fall asleep. The sounds and or the visuals cause a physiological response that invites a sensation of peace. It's what psychologists call a trigger.

In this context, triggers are emotional or mental stimulants. Unfortunately, some in modern therapy have regulated the word "trigger" to be one assigned with a negative connotation (i.e., they perceive triggers to be negative as they are discussed commonly in relation to PTSD and anger management, for example). Triggers are much more than that. Many times they can take us back to a life-impacting event in our minds. They are the internal parts of us that react to moments that stimulate something from our personal history that then causes us to react, change, and maybe even grow. In the scope of ASMR videos, the goals are more positive, leading us into serene modes, relieving our anxiety, and helping us get ready for rest.

This made so much sense on our last vacation. When my wife and I were hiking out west, we had a conversation about this phenomena without yet knowing much about ASMR. As we hiked along a stream, we were in the shadow of a mountain, working our way along a trail. Anne remarked how much the sound of water "soothes" her.

My wife loves to sit at the beach in the sun. She has zero intention of going in the water because she assumes something will *"eat her"* (yes, that is an exact quote). Being in the water doesn't do much for her, however, being near the water and listening to the waves crash or hearing the rushing of a river, calms her and *triggers* a sense of security and serenity.

Anne then remarked that sounds don't work for me like they do for her. For me, it's the mere sight of mountains that can transport me from a state of anxiety, almost as if flipping a switch, to a deep tranquility. Being in the presence of cliffs, ridges, and spires makes me smile and exhale as if I finally have permission to release any and all responsibilities connected to my life. In those moments, the rest of the world doesn't exist. For me, there's something about mountains that causes me to detach from life's stressors and take in the beauty of God's creation (not to mention it makes me want to grab my climbing equipment and start ascending up the crags). Like Anne with water, the sight of mountains trigger something inside of me that helps me let go of stress and embrace rest.

Goodbye home, hello Mayberry

My wife and I were hired as new Youth Pastors in 2002 for a church in mid-Michigan. This was a significant shift for us. First, we were eight months pregnant with our second child. Have you ever packed up a house during a pregnancy? Further, have you ever left your established doctors behind to give birth with a care team you've never met? Yep, it's not the easiest thing to do.

Secondly, we were moving away from family. Prior to the move, Anne's parents lived three miles away, and my folks lived a mere three blocks away. Anne and I were leaving our support network. Family wouldn't be close anymore. Even worse, now we actually had to pay for babysitters (love you mom and dad). To top it all off, we were leaving home in Metro Detroit to (what felt like to us) a tiny city of 36,000 people surrounded by corn fields. Anne would often say we were moving to Mayberry (yes, it's an Andy Griffith reference). In addition to the mentioned stressors, our new environment was also a massive shift in culture. What we didn't anticipate was that this new city would end up becoming much more than merely a job site. It became a city of refuge for our wounded souls.

Detroit was more than just what was "familiar." It was all we knew. It was our heritage. Other than going away to college, Southeast Michigan was where we were born and raised. It's where we met, got married, and started our family. What I didn't expect was how getting out of my natural element would bring to surface some of the brokenness that happened over the course of my life. Sometimes when you live in one place, one atmosphere, one environment, you can accumulate pain over time and not realize the depth of it. You can get so acclimated to some internal struggles that you don't understand how deep the roots of brokenness are settled in. Often, it's hard to recognize how unhealthy your life is until you experience something that is closer to what "healthy" really is. Even then, it takes time to become accustomed to living in that ethos, and even more time to restore your life towards becoming whole again.

If only all moments invited good memories

Can we all admit that everyone carries baggage? Left unhealed, your pain can be luggage you use to travel from one season of life to the next. Unless you get a realistic view of your life, you can unintentionally haul fracture, brokenness, and hurt from one place to another. This is what I experienced early in both my life and my ministry.

I didn't realize how significant this move would be. For the Barringers, this Mid-Michigan city will always be a special place. It would ultimately become a launching pad for us into becoming Lead Pastors so that we could bring the health we discovered into a local church that needed it. Until then, it would serve as both a cocoon and a potter's wheel. It was where I would be reborn from the hurts of my past and reshaped into what God truly intended.

I think of the story in the Scriptures when the Jewish people were led out of slavery into a new life of freedom. Even though they no longer had bondages on their wrists and feet, there were still shackles on their hearts, minds, and souls. Those years following their emancipation were filled with so many moments of longing to "*go back*" to the unhealthy life and atmosphere they were rescued out of. It seems that every moment of stress triggered their trauma and drew them mentally back into slavery. Why would people act that way? What would make someone want to go back to something so painful?

77

My thought: *Sometimes known slavery feels safer than unknown freedom.* Sometimes moments can trigger a mindset that can push us to resort back to a life of pain, just because it's "*all I know.*" It is more simple to behave in the way you originally learned than to put in the effort to overcome the trigger and automatic response. Simply said: Staying the same is easier than to do the hard work to establish a new norm.

Prior to our hiring, we had heard much about this church and their Lead Pastor. During the interview process, we couldn't believe how well we clicked. When we got there, what Anne and I saw in this new church, town, and the staff, it felt like a mirage. Everything looked and *seemed* authentic, but a part of me kept waiting for the moment when the "*other shoe was going to drop.*" Was this church going to live up to what we initially saw and the reputation it carried?

At this point no counselor had diagnosed me with depression. In my mind, "periodical sadness" was my norm and I had learned how to "deal with it." On top of that, the thought of getting help for the thoughts and feelings I was experiencing was humiliating. To me, this was a sign of weakness. Getting help, in my mind, was a way to affirm how inept I was at handling myself.

I was already on edge simply coming into the office on my first day as the Youth Pastor. I mean, who isn't nervous on their first day of work or school? You want to start off well and make a good impression. I got there early to get settled in, only to be promptly greeted by my new administrative assistant. I was told the staff wore business casual. She thought she'd mess with me and said, "*You're dressed a little casual.*" She paused and started laughing. I gave her a courtesy chuckle. On the inside, something started sinking. I was in the office for only a few minutes and panic was trying to seize my day.

Then my office intercom buzzed with the voice of my new Lead Pastor (also known as my boss!), saying in a stern voice, "*David, can I see you in my office?*" Those eight words triggered both physical and strong emotional responses in me. I started sweating as the panic increased. As ridiculous as it seems, the thought of "*how did I mess up already*" popped into my brain! The job isn't even ten minutes old and already I'm in trouble!

Even today, when I ask to meet with people, I'm told how nervous people get because *"When the Lead Pastor wants to talk to me, I'm very concerned. I must be in trouble if he's reached out to me."* Most, if not all the time, I just want to connect and encourage. I've been working for years to reverse this mindset. Nevertheless, the panic I see in people is visible and inevitable no matter how soft my approach. So while these feelings I was having, while very natural, were certainly amplified coming from not just our new Lead Pastor but my new boss.

The 30-foot journey down the hall suddenly became the longest walk of my life. I vividly remember sweating so profusely in those few seconds that I literally could see the sweat dripping off the tip of my nose. As I entered, he told me to shut the door behind me, intensifying my anxiety.

I sat in front of his desk and said, *"What's going on?"*

He paused, cracked a smile, and leaned across his desk to say, *"How did you think the Detroit Lions played yesterday?"*

I was dumbfounded by his question. I quickly replied, *"It doesn't matter. What do you need?"*

"David, that was all. I know you're a football fan. I am too. I just wanted your take on how you think the season would be."

I burst into tears in front of my new boss.

Looking back, I'm convinced that he had to be thinking to himself, *"What kind of mess is this man that I hired to lead our youth?!?"*

The stress of a new job. Living in unfamiliar surroundings. The little "joke" from my new coworker (likely done with the pure-hearted intention of helping me feel warmly welcomed by making a harmless joke). The stern voice over the speakerphone. By themselves, they can add some moments of anxiety. For someone with depression, these moments can be cataclysmic. For some people, these are minor occurrences that are somewhat normal or light-hearted. For someone dealing with depression, they were overwhelming. In hindsight, I see that my over-the-top emotional response came from repeated "triggers" being activated. My own mental health had left me with emotional trauma. The trauma left behind scars creating *triggers* that transformed average moments into painful ones. A joke should have been seen as just that. A fun way to welcome a new staff member. An attempt from my boss to connect with me should have been a huge encouragement. He was reaching out on a personal level but I couldn't detect it. I should have been flattered he knew I loved football. All I could detect was danger coming my way. Depression and its triggers left me with a callous over my soul to the point where I couldn't detect reality. Without my depression, these events may have actually hit their target to make me feel welcomed to the staff family in my new church.

You've got triggers, too?

There are a couple of things I want you to know about triggers. First, you don't have to deal with depression to have them. Humans naturally develop reflexes to instill a primal instinct to protect themselves. For example, if you get in a car accident while attempting to turn left, can you guess what's going to trigger an emotional response? Turning left. Have you met someone with a fear of dogs? Most likely, that person had a terrible experience with a dog at some point. When an unfamiliar dog approaches, a reflexive, protective response is *triggered*.

Second, triggers don't have to be a bad thing. There's a worker at our local grocery store who wears the same perfume as my grandmother. When I catch a whiff of it, my brain *"triggers"* memories of a simpler time, as a child, spending time at Grandma's. Similarly, when certain 80's songs play, they "trigger" internal responses in me that take me back to my childhood. *"Eye of the Tiger"* still takes me back to Rocky III with the desire to do the same workout Rocky is doing.

So, you can see, we all deal with *"triggers"* to some degree, and they don't have to be negative. They can involve any of the five senses and, sometimes, a combination of them. This may sound silly to some, but picking up pizza from a local place triggers all sorts of emotions. My dad used to take me to a place called "Pizza Joe's" near my childhood home. We would walk in and make our order instead of calling in. I'd pull up a chair so I could watch every step of the pizza being made. So the *sound* of the dough being slapped back and forth, the *smell* of the oven, *sight* of flour everywhere takes me back to a simpler time. To me, picking up pizza wasn't about dinner, it was some personal time with my dad.

As trivial as my example may seem to some, I say this to help you, the reader, not write triggers off or have you believe that only those of us who navigate the shadows possess them. I have triggers, and you have them too. My guess is that you've already thought of a few triggers that are both meaningful and challenging.

If you re-read the story of my first day on a new job, you'd recognize some of my triggers:

- Unfamiliar surroundings.

- The stress of a new job with more responsibilities.

- Being separated from my support network (family and friends).

- Being teased by a coworker.

- My "boss" needing to urgently speak with me without context.

- The solitary walk down an unfamiliar hall toward an authority figure.

They were all triggers, sending me reeling into all sorts of feelings and thoughts. "I have a fresh start. How come nothing has changed in me? I'm a mess. There's no way the Pastor is going to put up with me. Is this the way it's always going to be? Do I have to just get used to being like this?" I remember returning to my office, shutting the door, and wondering if there was any hope for healing.

There was.

And there's hope for you too.

I've come to an understanding in my life. If you still have breath in your lungs, God still has a plan. It's easy to preach that to people, but when you are in the thick of the darkness, it is extremely hard to believe it for yourself. In the face of what was triggering in me, there was a still small voice speaking to me, "There's still hope. There is still healing." Like wind blowing into a still sail, I knew it was the voice of God giving me the word I needed to hear to move me forward and raise my hope out of the darkness. What seemed to be a typical moment in the life of a depressed person (feeling crushed and trying to hope again) ended up being the catalyst for recognizing that there is a life of hope that could be more than a dream I had but a reality I could live.

There was still breath in me. That meant God wasn't done with me.

To you the reader, I want every breath you breathe to be a new trigger for you. I want every inhale of oxygen to be your reminder that God has a plan for you.

Keep pushing forward.

Keep trusting God.

Keep leaning into Him.

Keep stepping forward.

Watch what God can do in your life.

Are we seeing (or experiencing) the same thing?

Have you ever had a moment that invited happy feelings in some people but brought sadness or even emotional pain to others? As a pastor, I see this every year during most holidays, especially Mother's Day and Father's Day. While some celebrate with festivity, others mourn the moment. Perhaps it's the memory of a family member who had passed. Maybe the holiday reminds them of a time that *feels* better than the present. It could be a "reality check," shedding light on family connections or friendships that are not at peace. Regardless, it still astounds me how the duplicity of a single moment can invite both joy and sadness.

Enter Ezra, Chapter 3.

This portion of Scripture is out of one of those "forgotten" books of the bible that causes many church goers to need the table of contents to find it. It's not commonly accessed or quoted, yet there is so much depth to explore. Like much of Scripture, this narrative helps me to better understand how the same event can yield such a multitude of responses to individuals.

To give you some background, the Jewish people had been attacked by another nation. Their main city (Jerusalem) had been ransacked and their place of worship, the Temple, had been destroyed by an invading nation. The defeated people were then led into captivity for 70 years. After that time of exile, they've finally returned to Jerusalem. As life began to settle and they traveled back into their home city, the people began to rebuild the Temple by laying the foundation. Something peculiar happened when the people saw the foundations of the Temple being laid. Two reactions took place.

...And all the people shouted with a great shout when they praised the Lord, because the foundation of the house of the Lord was laid. But many of the priests and Levites and heads of fathers' houses, old men who had seen the first house, wept with a loud voice when they saw the foundation of this house being laid, though many shouted aloud for joy, so that the people could not distinguish the sound of the joyful shout from the sound of the people's weeping, for the people shouted with a great shout, and the sound was heard far away.

Ezra 3:11-13 ESV

Did you see it? Joy and sadness over the same event. What brought jubilation to many invited inner pains from a broken past. What brought out these diverse emotional reactions? Let us explore...

Everyone who had been born during the 70-year captivity shouted and celebrated. Why? They returned to the home of their forefathers, and they got to participate in the rebuilding of their place of worship. Imagine being a part of a couple of generations who had heard of the opulence of the former Temple and its city. Now, as the rebuild starts, excitement begins to build as the foundation gets laid. This is the moment when you think, *"Life just gets better and better."*

Amidst all this excitement and forward momentum, there was another group who reacted much differently. This was the group born prior to the captivity. They were old enough to remember the city and its Temple, in their original glory. The younger contingent didn't know what they had lost. It's hard to miss something you've never had. This older group knew all too well what was stolen and destroyed. They felt it deeply. Instead of celebrating what they regained, all they could think of was what had been ripped from them.

A reminder that we are talking about the foundation. Not a wall had been built nor a pillar erected. It was just the foundation. That simple, flat piece of stone became the trigger, taking these folks to a time of incredible trauma, trauma from a memory 70+ years before that became so fresh they cried out. These *"priests and Levites and heads of fathers' houses, old men who had seen the first house"* were going through multiple levels of pain. Dependent on the individual, this moment likely triggered thoughts of:

- Mourning: *I remember what/who we lost.*
- Agony: *I'm reliving the whole incident.*
- Self-reflection: *Maybe we could have done something to prevent this?*
- Anger at God: *Why did God allow this?*
- Fascination: *What would life be like if we hadn't gone through that?*
- Shame: *I/we caused that to happen.*
- Regret: *Why do I get to live while so many others didn't?*
- Hopelessness: *Will we ever get back what we had?*
- Fearful: *If it happened before, it could happen again.*
- Bitterness: *Can I ever see them (those who captured them) and not be hateful?*

Remember, a "trigger" is nothing more than something that sets off a feeling, a memory, or a moment of trauma. For this older group, the foundation of their house of worship invited back the anguish that had potentially been buried for decades. Until a trauma is healed, it lingers in the background waiting for a trigger to reopen the door to make its grand reappearance.

Ezra 3 is all too real to me. I know what it's like to think I've moved forward past an issue only for the tone of a voice, a phrase uttered, a song played, an event attended, or a personality type experienced, to tether me back to a moment that seemed long gone. Then, while people around me seem to be enjoying life, I'm crying out in pain (often, internally), unable to keep myself together. People seem to be able to move forward, yet I'm shackled to an event I didn't ask for or invite to happen to me.

They, "*wept with a loud voice when they saw the foundation of this house being laid…*"

I find it fascinating that the Temple's foundation was the trigger. Instead of seeing it as the bedrock for a better future, it became the launch pad for unresolved past pain. I can imagine the looks on most people's faces seeing the older generation weeping. I've seen people look at me the same way.

Confused. Shocked. Concerned. Weirded out. Judgmental.

I've seen people trying to figure out why my enthusiasm for the moment or a lack of positivity didn't match their own. What they don't know is that the trigger has changed the filter of how I see life. One moment has adjusted my perspective to view things from a new angle that I can't quite shake. You see, just because an event has passed, doesn't mean a wound has healed.

I have seen people walk away not knowing what to do with me. Some have gotten angry and/or frustrated with me. Others have gossiped about me whether or not I have the emotional make-up to be in the vocation I'm in. I'll admit, most respond with compassion and kindness even though they don't know what to do nor understand what is going on inside of me. I'm grateful for those who've tried to reach out despite their lack of experience or exposure with depression.

So how does this end? This is the part of Ezra 3 I wish existed. The chapter ends with this dichotomy of emotions, and we don't know what was the result. We do know that ultimately the Temple was finished but we never hear how this moment concluded. My guess: the plethora of celebratory voices overshadowed the sorrowful ones. The attention went to the majority that found joy in the moment. For those who were hurting (and I realize this is complete conjecture), most likely they tried to bury it deeper in their hearts, hoping to just cope with the moment and move on. For many of us that deal with the shadows, it seems like it's our only resort. Like we are shackled to life events from our past and can't be freed of the characteristics that created that moment.

The good news: There's a better way to handle triggers. You don't have to bury them, nor do you have to sit and tolerate them. I believe we can find healing for them. In order to do this, you must be willing to allow light to shine in the darkness.

Call out your feelings

I've heard two schools of thought in the church world about feelings. One is to completely ignore them — as if feelings are the result of sin and not a God-given gift. In other words, don't listen to your feelings because they'll lead you astray. While this can happen, it is certainly not the hard rule concerning emotions. The second common historical misconception in the church is to buy into your feelings completely as if they are the ones in charge. You may hear something like, "*go with what you feel; follow your heart.*" Don't get me wrong, feelings are very important as they are the sounding board of what's happening in our soul, but to have every human solely live by every whim of every emotion would be more destructive than a zombie apocalypse hitting our world. Imagine everyone doing or saying what they felt in the moment without any logic or moral compass (Yikes!!). Again, this strategy can become counter-productive and even destructive.

I want to give you an alternate approach. I'm going to ask you to stay with me here as it may sound very unorthodox. *Call out your feelings; name them out loud.* The identification of your emotions does two things. First, it verbalizes what is happening on the inside. I've heard it said that your feelings are like the indicator lights on the dashboard of your vehicle. Those warning lights you see don't drive the car, they tell you what's happening under the hood. Verbalizing what you are feeling and why you are feeling that way is using the full capacity of the frontal lobe of your brain. That part of your cerebrum exists to detect emotions, yet it is also used for reasoning. Use both.

The processing of translating what you are feeling into words will lead you toward the second reason for this approach. Naming our emotions will begin the process of determining where these feelings originated from. Just like geologists and archaeologists use carbon dating to figure out the age of fossils, processing your emotions may help identify when (and perhaps why) the pain originally happened. This has helped me understand that the strong emotion I may currently be feeling may come as a result from a wound of the past that I have not allowed to properly heal. Since I haven't allowed healing from the previous trauma, the present day becomes inflicted with past hurt.

As you can see, identifying your feelings is so much more complex than simply admitting you're feeling sad or angry. It helps you process what you're experiencing through discovering the emotion's genesis. You are owning your feelings and getting to the roots of their beginnings. When you do that, the healing process can begin.

Invite Jesus into the pain.

In Scripture, the first miracle of Christ is recorded in the second chapter of the book of John. Jesus is at a wedding and turns water into wine when He is approached on behalf of the host family about a desperate cultural situation. The need is presented to Him and He responds by helping them avoid being shamed in front of their guests. Have you ever wondered why Jesus was at the wedding in the first place? (I'll give you a hint, it's the same reason why people show up to weddings today.)

He was invited.

It's really that simple. An invitation is given. He responds to it with His presence. I know what you're thinking, just because someone receives an invitation doesn't assure they'll show up.

Let's get this straight: Jesus isn't "other people." His presence is *promised* to all who call out to Him. A simple invitation makes all the difference. Yet the things that are considered "simple" are certainly not always "easy." When I'm dealing with my shadows, I don't even want to be around myself. So if I do ask Jesus to come into these feelings or into my experience, it makes me wonder why would he want to accept that invitation?

Psalm 145:18 NLT says, "*The LORD is close to all who call on him, yes, to all who call on him in truth.*" I love the ending of that Scripture. He comes close to those who cry out to Him *in truth*. There is something special in being vulnerable enough to be truthful about what we're dealing with. When we've taken the boldness to identify our feelings and own them, when we put words to our visceral responses, it allows us to be truthful about the realities of the pain we're in. So often, I've seen people put on a mask to pretend things are alright. Perhaps they've grown up in an atmosphere where being vulnerable wasn't okay or acceptable. Maybe they believe the lie, "fake it till you make it" and put on a brave face amidst internal struggle while anxiously awaiting a better tomorrow.

With Christ, being truthful about our pain is not just the recognition of what we are dealing with, but the admission that we cannot deal with it alone. It's out of our "truthfulness" that Jesus comes "close" to us. The question then rises, "*Why wasn't God close before the pain?*"

The simple answer: He was.

One of the most repeated promises of the Bible is the assurance of His presence. It doesn't matter what you are facing or what you are going through, you don't have to worry about God's whereabouts. He is with you. I love the words of the Psalmist who said,

> *"I can never escape from your Spirit! I can never get away from your presence!*
> *If I go up to heaven, you are there; if I go down to the grave, you are there.*
> *If I ride the wings of the morning, if I dwell by the farthest oceans, even there your hand will guide me, and your strength will support me.*
> *I could ask the darkness to hide me and the light around me to become night—*
> *but even in darkness I cannot hide from you.*
> *To you the night shines as bright as day.*
> *Darkness and light are the same to you."*

Psalm 139:7-12 NLT

Truth Trumps Feelings

When I'm going through depression, there are moments where it seems I can't sense God's presence. Have you been there? Have you been in the place where you are craving that sensation where you feel the nearness of His presence? It seems that mechanism within me that is aware of God is not working. In those moments, He doesn't feel close at all. That may not seem like a huge deal to some, but for those of us who navigate the *shadows*, the feeling of aloneness can become paralyzing. On top of that, the inner darkness makes us emotionally numb to feeling anything whatsoever. Like having a car with transmission problems, my depression makes it challenging to "shift" into a gear that recognizes and connects to the presence of God. When you can't feel His presence, you lean into feeling abandoned.

To combat this *feeling*, I stick to a cardinal rule of dealing with my shadows: *truth trumps feelings*.

If the truth is God is always with me, it doesn't matter if I feel Him there,

I KNOW He's there.

If I don't see any evidence of Him being around or within me,

I KNOW He's there.

If people abandon me because they don't know how to deal with my darkness,

I KNOW He's there.

It's in those moments when I must keep reminding myself: God's presence is not dictated by my senses. He is there whether I feel Him or not.

So why does Psalm 145 (NLT) say He is *"close to all who call on him in, yes, to all who call on him in truth"*? First, I'd contend that when our emotional turmoil is present, we feel God is absent because that's what we expect of others. It feels as if everyone is going to leave us. *Why would God, or anyone, want to be around a mess like me?* When our inner pain is present, God seems far away. My friend, no statement could be further from the truth.

This leads me to my second thought: God makes His presence known to us. He draws us close to Him. I remember the days of my daughter being small and scared of thunderstorms. She'd cry out and I would go into her room and say *"Everything is going to be okay. It's just a storm."* She didn't want me to simply stand nearby. She needed me closer. I'd hear her say,

"Daddy, come here."

"I am here. I'm literally standing 5 feet away."

"I need to feel you near. Come hold my hand."

I'd kneel down next to her bed and she'd cuddle up next to me and close her eyes. My presence did nothing to alter the course of the storm itself. My presence did, however, change the storm inside her. There's something about our pain that makes God go from simply "being in the room" with us, to coming nearer to us to better help us through our internal storm.

God isn't detoured by our pain. He isn't offended by it. Our hurts don't scare Him, nor do they push Him away. God doesn't avoid us when we are in our *shadows*. In fact, He comes into the middle of them to meet us there. He brings himself close to us.

From personal experience, my challenge and advice to you is when pain or trauma has been triggered, call out to God and invite Him into it. The key is: You must be *truthful* about it. Be vulnerable with Him and admit with a humble heart that you don't have it all together. Jesus doesn't show up for the pretend version of yourself that you altered for your post on social media, designed and filtered for the likes of your followers. Jesus wants to show up for the real version of you that needs His presence. Those invites are the ones He never turns down.

Develop healthy margins

In high school, I took an architecture course (back in the day, known as drafting). We began every project by marking off the borders of each page to develop a margin to work within. This helps to center your work and to set the layout of your drawings. This simple, yet important step, sets up the project to look balanced on the page and assure that you do not run out of space from working too close to the edge.

Margins are all about creating that healthy space to work in. They not only aid in creating a clean architectural drawing, but margins help to bring healing to a life triggered by trauma. When I'm done processing what is going on in my soul and identifying my emotions, I recognize that there are areas that need to be developed in order for healing to take place.

Let's be real, we all need breathing room; free spaces in our life to be able to take a collective emotional, mental, physical, and spiritual breath. Think about your own triggers that may have led you to feeling discouraged, downcast, or even depressed. Sometimes people get so busy living in the moment, day-to-day, with zero margin, they don't realize the daily situations or circumstances which trigger their depressive mood. People, places, ideas, and events, all influence your mental health differently. Even though we've taken the critical step of identifying our feelings, something must be done about the everyday-ness of life in order that we don't continue to live in the destructive wake of our triggers. Developing margins is a great next step.

Margins are all about creating space between the load you carry and the limits you have. If you are exceeding the borders of your physical, emotional, mental, and/or spiritual well-being, you will continue to get bombarded with your triggers and, thus, risk burnout. Margins construct a safe space to catch your breath, and establish a consistent place to breathe. With so much demanding our attention and so many demanding our time, our culture doesn't lend toward the space to create "healthy" margins. Marriages, careers, or parenting alone can consume so much of our weekly lives that it feels like there is little time left to maintain the health of your soul.

I need you to understand three things about margins. First, *everyone needs them.* They're not just for those of us with triggers. Margins are foundational for a healthy life. Second, *they are very personal and individual.* What you set up for your personal health may or may not look like somebody else's. We are all individuals, each fearfully and wonderfully made by God. Humans are a species with diverse backgrounds that carry diverse needs. Which leads me to my last point, *margins can be complex.* If your trigger has roots in deeper trauma, the margins you build in your life may be wider in scope (i.e., more guarded) than others.

For example, a few years ago I was rock climbing in Kentucky. While 40 feet up on the side of a mountain, I was reaching up to clip my rope higher when my left foot slipped and I fell 15 feet onto a small granite cliff. It was such an awkward and terrible fall that my belay partner didn't know if I was knocked out or if the fall had killed me. It was by far the worst fall that I've ever had rock climbing. From that day, over the next 3-4 months, my climbing was inhibited by the trauma from that moment. My body needed a week or so to heal. My mentality however, took longer than that. The incident didn't stop me from climbing but I did provide a wider scope to what I climb and how I climb it. I had to create some margin based upon what I experienced mixed with what I needed to do to get healthier. My approach to climbing had to shift for a season as to get both mind and body whole.

Triggers are easy to trip when life is lived without limits. Like being stuck in the middle seat on a plane in which the people on either side of you are taking up both of your armrests, margin-less lives stifle any opportunity to enjoy or engage in the journey you are on. Once you intentionally develop and maintain personal margins, you can begin the process of identifying your triggers and finding healing.

Get some trigger help.

In the hit Broadway production, "Hamilton," there is a song called "Meet me inside" where George Washington is trying to have a conversation with Alexander Hamilton. It's a meeting of two great minds. However, the motivation of the meeting is not for collaboration, rather for intervention. General Washington is trying to preserve Alexander's life. He addresses him as "*Son*" in which Hamilton replies with "*Don't call me son.*"

Tension builds.

Five lines later, to get his attention, the general again says, "*Son…*" in which Alexander interrupts with, "*I'm not your son.*"

Tension rises.

Nine lines later, voices are louder. Faces are more stern. "*Your wife needs you alive son, I need you alive…*"

"*Call me son one more time…*"

The moment is so powerful. You really catch that this character has had something within him building up to the point where he explodes on the one person for whom being called "son" should be an honor. This is the general of generals. This is a man whom people to this day idolize and admire. Hamilton can't hear the honor in "son." He only hears the hurt from his orphaned life. Of all the moments for him to be triggered, this is the worst time. He's in front of his commanding officer, his mentor, and perhaps his only father-figure. But that's what pain does. It doesn't care who the person is nor the moment at hand. Pain simply wants an excuse to be present.

If there's anything I've learned is ignoring issues never really helped anyone. You need to attend to the triggers so that you can move forward. I've heard people say, "*Just avoid your triggers and you'll be fine.*" Sounds like great advice until you realize ignoring them not only fortifies the triggers but it delays your healing.

Let's look at some real-world examples:

As a pastor, I've seen people so hurt by church that the idea of talking to a pastor or going to church triggers all sorts of feelings. The problem is that faith grows best in community. This is more than personal opinion but biblical fact. Simply staying away from being in a congregation because of triggers doesn't help you get emotionally healthy or spiritually healthy. In fact, it can quarantine you from an opportunity to find healing and develop meaningful relationships.

Another example, you may have grown up treated in a way that says you can't be vulnerable with your ideas and opinions. A big part of healthy communication with friendships and relationships is the willingness to listen to others and the boldness to share your thoughts. However, because of your past, your opinions and feelings were shut down by others. You were not listened to and your feelings were not validated. When you did share, you were always made to feel "wrong." Disengaging from people altogether doesn't prevent triggers from happening, it leaves you isolated and alone.

A last example could be something like sexual abuse in your past. A healthy part of marriage is healthy sex and intimacy. Now that you are thinking about getting married (or are married), there is this fear of being intimate because of what had happened to you. So staying away from sex in your marriage doesn't stop the triggers, it withholds sexual enjoyment and fulfillment from the both of you.

Now obviously, this isn't an exhaustive list. For many people, there are a load of everyday moments that can send them into yesterday's pain. Ignoring the trigger doesn't invite healing but it delays wholeness. My challenge to you is to seek help on two fronts that you can do simultaneously.

First, lean into the Lord. As stated, inviting Christ into your pain is to introduce the ultimate healing agent into the festering wound so that infection halts and deep healing begins. We are physical beings as well as spiritual beings. To disconnect them from each other is to not understand that one affects the other. Start taking this to the Lord in prayer and make it a matter of allowing His presence to help usher in healing.

While leaning into Jesus, lean into a solid counselor or therapist. While I'm a man of faith, I recognize that God has given gifts to this world in the form of doctors, nurses, and clinicians. I'm a better human being because of amazing professionals speaking into my life. You need to remind yourself that one appointment won't make everyone better. It just gets you on the road to getting whole. It will take you a couple sessions just to establish connection and trust with the counselor or therapist. If you don't connect, don't give up on counseling. Find one you do connect with.

Do you have triggers? Me too.

Can you get healing for them? I did. You can too.

Make a decision today that triggers are no longer going to rule your life by getting the help and the healing you deserve. Today is your day for taking a step forward. I pray that this chapter is the *trigger* you need to move you ahead.

Survival Tips for the Shadows:
Change Your Punctuation.

Punctuation is something that seems automatic. Most of us don't think much about it when we send messages. That said, punctuation adds clarity and precision to your writing. It can bring a statement to a full stop, or it can insert a pause in order to change up the flow. For example:

"*Let's eat Dave.*" and, "*Let's eat*, Dave."

If you say the first sentence, I'm going to be a bit concerned about my well-being. If you add a comma, then I'm ready to join you for tacos or some shawarma.

Why is this a "survival tip for the shadows"?

Many times our depression wants to put a "period" at the end of a moment, a feeling, or a thought. In punctuation terms, a "period" is used to end a statement or thought.

You are depressed. Period. Full Stop.

You will never get better. Period. Full Stop.

You'll never be happy again. Period. Full Stop.

Let me introduce you to an "ellipsis." An ellipsis is signified by three dots and indicates that there is more to be said. I'd even encourage you to verbalize an "ellipsis" by using the word "yet."

I'm not healed…yet.

I can't feel joy…yet.

I can't see the light at the end of the tunnel…yet.

I want to get you in a mode of seeing your life through the eyes of faith in Christ that truly knows that the best has yet to come for your life. So, if life hands you a "period," replace it with an "ellipses." God's not done with you! There's more for your life. Maybe it just hasn't happened…yet.

– 6 –

IYKYK

When I thought I lost me
You knew where I left me
You reintroduced me to Your love
You picked up all my pieces
Put me back together
You are the defender of my heart

"Defender" by Rita Springer

"The Lord is a shelter for the oppressed, a refuge in times of trouble."

Psalm 9:9 NLT

I'm a movie guy. I'd take a movie any day over a show. I think part of it is that I can get closure in 2 hours instead of having to endure anywhere from 8-24 episodes to get some sort of relief to the tension that an entire season of television creates. Even though I'm a movie guy, I do have a few go-to television shows I will watch over and over. My wife doesn't understand why I'd rather rewatch something familiar than jump into something new. It was a mystery to me until I heard someone say that new and unexpected storylines can cause stress and some people like the safety of knowing what to expect while trying to catch a new detail.

That's me.

One of my favorite go-to series, for which many critics would rate it as one of the greatest television shows of all time, is the West Wing. I'm not very politically inclined but I do love its humor, drama, and pace of story. The man who birthed the show, Aaron Sorkin, is a genius at writing fast dialogue and developing characters that millions of people still love and watch. The show was so masterfully done, it caught the attention of the actual White House and its employees.

Yes, I'm a West Wing Nut. Amongst many of the storylines over the seven seasons, there's one line that sticks out to me because it hits home with my depression. This line is how I helped my wife better understand my mentality while I'm dealing with the shadows.

"I'm not sure you were fully conscious while you were saying it."

Humor me for a moment as I paint the background of this brilliant line that means so much to me.

A character named Josh Lyman has survived a gunshot from domestic terrorists. Though he is back at work after physically recouping from the incident, there is something obvious about him that isn't quite whole. His mental and emotional healing hasn't mended at the rate of his physical body. We get to see this played out in an episode in the second season called "*Noel.*"

The scene shows Josh talking to a traumatologist named Stanley Keyworth. Stanley has been probing Josh with questions about the peculiarity of his demeanor around his co-workers, who are concerned. The most concerning moment happened in the Oval Office, where Josh raised his voice to the President of the United States. Of course Josh denies being out of sorts until Stanley pushes harder. We are then invited into a flashback of that specific meeting to reveal what Josh was clearly suppressing.

What should have been a casual meeting with the President and a few advisors has grown more intense by the second as Josh's tone gets sharper and his disposition intensifies. Josh became verbally and emotionally out of control. Both Josh's superior (Leo) and his good friend (Sam) are trying to stop him in the midst of his rant when all of a sudden, Josh yelled at the President, "*Just listen to me!*" The actor, Brad Witford, did a brilliant job of showing us that his character is being driven by something other than the topic at hand. His performance was so stellar that he won an Emmy for this episode.

We head into 11 seconds of silence (on screen this feels like an eternity), with the only sound effects being the clock and an emotionally exhausted character breathing heavily. Josh is dismissed to wait in the Chief of Staff's office so the meeting can conclude, until Leo can join him.

LEO: *You're gonna sit with a guy.*

JOSH: *Leo...*

LEO: *You're gonna sit with a guy.*

JOSH: *If this is because of what I just said in there, I wasn't at my best with...*

LEO: *(interrupts) Josh, I'm not sure you were fully conscious while you were saying it.*

"This is what it's like"

Most of the chapters in this book have begun with a personal story. While not a story from my own life, the excerpt I shared from the West Wing here is still extremely personal to me as it's the way I helped my wife better understand me and my journey through depression. I can tell you exactly where we were on our neighborhood walk when I used this scene to paint a picture of what *"living in the shadows" is like.*

Being depressed is as if you are unconscious and awake at the same time.

Simply put, when I'm living in the shadows, I'm completely wide awake physically but "unconscious" or emotionally numb to what I'm actually doing. I'm interacting or responding yet I'm not nearly as aware of what is happening around or inside of me, as compared to my alertness and absorption during times that the depression is in check. It feels surreal, and is certainly hard to articulate what exactly is happening. I almost consider it akin to an out-of-the-body experience.

I mean, IYKYK (**If You Know You Know**). If you don't, then you're probably thinking I've lost my mind.

During these moments, I've hurt people's feelings while not grasping what I was doing or saying. I've had people angry at me thinking I was "ghosting" them when I didn't even realize I was withdrawn. At one point, I tried to describe it like a scene from the movie "Dr. Strange" where the "astral form" leaves the body and interacts apart from the natural universe. There's nothing mystical about it. It's just dreamlike. Clinicians will call it depersonalization; the feeling of observing yourself from outside yourself. I see myself doing things, acting certain ways, and I feel completely helpless to do anything about it. For example:

I can't detect the tone of my voice and don't realize how I come off to others.

I don't understand how my attitude is affecting those around me.

I don't notice or acknowledge people near to me.

I can't detect other people's needs or even their concerns.

I tend to say things without thought or filter.

I project an ethos that says, "stay away from me" when I really need people in the moment.

What's worse: I don't always remember my conduct in these situations. When I do, it only intensifies the darkness as shame and guilt weigh even more heavily on me. So, when Leo says, *"I'm not sure you were fully conscious while you were saying it.,"* it hits me hard and reminds me of the struggle that is all too real to me.

A friend of mine who is a licensed therapist once gave me a picture of an MRI of two brains that were at the Mayo Clinic. One scan showed a brain with normal brain activity. It was lit up with all sorts of color and movement. The other scan was of a person who was in a state of depression. It was astounding how little function was happening in the brain. Both brains were people who were both awake. Both brains were people who were both physically healthy. The difference between the individuals was a depressed brain versus a non-depressed brain and the visual showed how brain function is stifled during times of depression.

Explanations and not excuses.

I've hurt my marriage through my depression. It breaks my heart how much of an inconvenience it has brought to our home. I have spent too many days in silence, hurting, not realizing how what I was projecting to my wife and my kids. I recall an instance where, out of instinct, I'd leaned over to my wife in bed to put my arm around her because I needed to feel her close to me only to hear,

"Oh, now you want to be nice. You want to be kind now that you want something from me."

I wasn't asking for sex. Quite frankly, I really didn't know what I wanted. I only knew what I needed: to physically feel my wife nearby. While I can't **excuse** my behavior leading to that moment, I can do my best to **explain** it.

This lack of self-awareness is something many of us deal with in our depression. For me, it happens more often than I'd like. When it's present, I can be completely unaware of, or numb to, the things I'm doing and how I'm coming across to those closest to me. It's almost like becoming an emotional zombie, for lack of better illustration. I've got my life force driving me yet nothing coherently directing me. Like a zombie with this primal instinct to eat, when we are hurting, we act out of our own basic instincts. For most of us, our basic instincts can be seen in how we convey our "Love Languages."

I love talking about the "Love Languages." The concept of them came from the book called "Five Love Languages" by Gary Chapman. If you've never read the book, the premise is simple: every one of us operates out of five different love languages. The five are quality time, acts of service, physical touch, words of affirmation, and gifts. According to the book we all have primary love languages and are spoken and received more than others. For example, my primary love language has always been physical touch. Even though love languages can change through the years, mine has always been steadily "touch." What happens is when someone is in their points of pain, depending on who the person is, they'll resort to the love languages they know best. It's what they'll crave in their darkest moment.

Looking back, I put my arm around my wife because I was hurting and needed the comfort of her nearness. I was reaching out of my most basic instinct, my top love language. It's what my body knew to do to respond to the internal pain and to cope with my agony. Physically reaching out was my default.

It was the next day when we went on a walk together and had a conversation about the events of that week. It was there she heard my West Wing story. That was the moment she finally understood. I was not fully "awake" that week. I wasn't fully conscious. I *seemed* to be functioning outwardly, but inwardly, I was completely numb.

You may be thinking, "*Are you just giving an excuse for people to be rude or hurtful when they're depressed?*" Not at all. **I'm not trying to excuse the behavior. I am trying to explain it.** For those of us who deal with depression, we would give anything to get moments back that we ruined with our attitude and demeanor. We wince at the memories of lost conversations and connections by our actions, even though, in the moment, we couldn't comprehend what we were doing. I mean, IYKYK. To everyone we've frustrated and pushed away, we ask for your patience, your continual love, your understanding, and PLEASE, your continued friendship. It's not easy dealing with our shadows. We also know, it's not easy dealing with us.

I do want to recognize that there are some of you who are reading currently who have never dealt with depression but who are married to, related to, or are friends with someone close who has treated you poorly while going through the shadows. It has hurt you severely. Your trust in them may be broken. The relationship is probably strained. Concern over your connection to them is at an all-time high. As someone who's caused pain unintentionally through these moments, I'd be the very first to ask for your forgiveness. The pain they caused wasn't malicious. It was out of their own hurt, much like a reactive wounded animal.

If your friend or loved one knew what he/she was doing, they would stop it in a heartbeat. They hurt over what they have caused and the shame of what they're enduring buries the angst over what they've inflicted on others. None of this is an excuse for the damage. It's just an explanation in hopes that with some of this insight, you may be able to find forgiveness and perhaps even consider reconnecting with them. Listen, we who deal with depression want to do better. We can do better. It can be very isolating living life when, in seasons of it, you feel so numb.

I've Become So Numb

Numb is a word I've used so often to describe what I'm going through on the inside. In 2003, Linkin Park released a song called "Numb" in which part of the chorus reads,

"I've become so numb
I can't feel you there"

I remember fixating on those lyrics for weeks. A song dedicated to describing a child frustrated at the weight of their parents' expectations became my anthem for a tough season. I was coherent as far as being awake and alive, but all the *feels* that make a day or relationships enjoyable were seemingly absent. I was, simply put, numb.

Emotional numbness can be a symptom of depression. We feel numb to everything around us and everything inside of us. It can leave us feeling totally disconnected from the world. When you experience this emotional numbness, it can come off as if you've become an empty vessel; a shell of a person. You'll feel empty yet you will somehow simultaneously feel overwhelmingly weighed down. Moments that usually bring about emotion can leave us feeling absolutely nothing at all.

It's almost as if we're living in an invisible bubble that we can feel is there. It prevents us from being impacted or touched by events and situations that would normally elicit a response. We feel disconnected from people, life experiences, and even our own bodies. If we don't feel any connection, this positions us to isolate ourselves from others. Why is this so? In our minds, we've become invisible to the world around us; unimportant and unnecessary. As a result, we tend to close ourselves off. Alternatively, we might find things to do in an attempt to feel *something*.

There is a relevant story in Scripture, one that I was hesitant to include in this book. My concern lies in the nature of the man's oppression. He is known as a man who is possessed by demons. Before I give you the story, I want to be VERY CLEAR: I am in NO way attributing depression to demon possession. I've heard people assign the stigma of demonic possession to both myself and to others who experience mental health issues. Even though the darkness we face is *oppressive*, it is a drastic difference than the evil darkness that is *possessive*.

"Demonic," or just "damaged"?

The story is both tragic and triumphant as it talks about a man who's been tormented by inner darkness. As goes in the book of Mark:

> *When Jesus climbed out of the boat, a man possessed by an evil (or unclean) spirit came out from the tombs to meet him. This man lived in the burial caves and could no longer be restrained, even with a chain. Whenever he was put into chains and shackles—as he often was—he snapped the chains from his wrists and smashed the shackles. No one was strong enough to subdue him. Day and night he wandered among the burial caves and in the hills, howling and cutting himself with sharp stones.*

Mark 5:4-5 NLT

There is much depth to the few details given. My breakdown of this passage includes the following points:

• This man was clearly dealing with massive internal darkness.

• He lived amongst the dead.

• Living amidst the dead, he was, by ceremonial laws of the time, declared unclean.

• As he was "unclean", he would have been spiritually ostracized from God and his community.

• The only way his community knew to deal with him was to abandon him, leaving him alone bound up (rather than giving him help and hope).

• He wandered in places where there is no life.

• While we were provided with all these details, we don't even get to know him by his name. We only know him by his condition.

A few years ago, I was preparing for a sermon out of this passage, and I found myself connected with him on an emotional level.

• I too was experiencing internal darkness.

• I had been living life feeling so numb, I felt like I was the walking dead.

• I felt ostracized from God because I couldn't "sense" Him.

• My family and community didn't know what to do with me.

• I was known to everyone as distant, silent, and withdrawn.

• I wandered aimlessly onto websites, social media, and other activities, which blankly occupied my time but where there was nothing life-giving.

Then I caught a detail that I felt I had misunderstood up until that point. I've read this passage regularly, my entire life, yet suddenly, verse 5 leapt right off the page.

> *"…he wandered among the burial caves and in the hills, howling and cutting himself with sharp stones."*

I grew up viewing this portion of the passage to emphasize that this man was trying to destroy his body; he appeared suicidal. At the time I interpreted that this man was so possessed that the demons inside of him were trying to kill him, or that he was so out of his mind that he was trying to end his life.

Let me offer another train of thought: he wasn't trying to *end* his life but rather trying to *feel* alive.

"I want to feel alive."

Years ago, I sat in a conference to learn about how to help hurting teenagers. One of the difficult topics we learned about was "self-harm." This could include cutting, burning, or poking the skin. When the speaker walked us through the issue, she said something fascinating.

"Cutters cut to feel, not to kill."

I couldn't let it go. In fact, this is all my leadership team could talk about following the conference. While we hadn't previously understood the topic of self-harm as well as we'd have liked to, the way the speaker presented it made so much sense. When a person inflicts harm upon themselves, it's not necessarily to punish themselves. It may be simply to "feel" human. For some, self harm can simply be a suffering soul's way of breaking out of the numbness by using physical pain as a way to feel human; it's a way to feel alive again.

When people cut themselves, it can be likened to a form of self-medication. Their life is numb. They have no feeling. Those who harm themselves will talk about feeling relief, a high, a connectedness, or a calming sensation. The pain causes the brain to release protective endorphins, which become the "payoff" for the pain. Personally, I didn't fully understand this until I got my first tattoo. When I got home, my wife asked me how bad it hurt. I remember saying, *"It was more enjoyable than painful. I feel relaxed."* I told her that for the first time, I got a *glimpse* of why cutters cut themselves. I also understood why people get addicted to tattoos. It's more than just artistic expression. It's the physical sensation and the release they receive. I mean, IYKYK.

Now think again about the man in our biblical story. He *"wandered* among the burial caves and in the hills, howling and cutting himself with sharp stones." Was he suicidal after all? I really don't think so. Destroying the body may have been on a demon's mind, but it wasn't on his. What was he thinking? Signs point toward him wanting to feel human again. While other people saw him trying to destroy himself, perhaps he was actually crying out for help. Remember, cutters cut to feel, not to kill. This man wanted to feel relief from his internal, emotional pain by experiencing one of the most basic human sensations: pain.

Sometimes you may feel so numb that ANY feeling is better than the lack of feeling. I'm not advocating or encouraging self-harm. In fact, I would highly discourage it. However, I describe this to bring you into the world of those of us who feel numb and long to experience what "normal" humans experience. Reading this story genuinely breaks my heart. It's more than the fact that he's cut himself. It's that his lifestyle and his world of darkness was all he had known. He was stuck in a mode that he couldn't break out of. As a result, he became nothing more than a "battery chicken."

Battery Chickens

I'm a fan of watching cooking shows. I've got several favorite chefs, but at the top of the list comes Jamie Oliver. Perhaps it's his particular style of cooking, or the rustic way he presents it. Maybe it's his English accent narrating his work (well, probably all three), but I'm absolutely enthralled by everything he creates in the kitchen. He has been on a crusade in the UK to wean his country off what he calls "battery chickens." This term comes from hens that are confined in "battery cages" for the dismal duration of their lives. The obvious difference between these factory-raised "egg producers," and free-range hens is their ability to move about cage-free, to be able to spread their wings, stretch out, and lay their eggs in nests.

On his show, "Jamie at Home," he brought out a "battery hen" he had rescued from an egg production facility. He set the hen out in an open space but it wouldn't move. It didn't walk away nor flap its wings. The only experience the chicken had for the entirety of its life was the walls of a cage that was barely bigger than its body. There was no reason to move because its mind told it there was no space to move. It seems silly as we look from the outside telling it to join the flock or to peck at the ground like the other chickens. Why would it? Whether or not it remains in a physical cage, its mind still remains in captivity.

Back to our story:

When Jesus was still some distance away, the man saw him, run to meet him, and bowed low before him. With a shriek, he screamed, "Why are you interfering with me, Jesus, Son of the Most High God? In the name of God, I beg you, don't torture me!" Then Jesus demanded,

"What is your name?"

And he replied, "My name is Legion, because there are many of us inside this man."

Mark 5:6-9 NLT

The immediate observation many notice is the name, "Legion." In that culture, the word meant a "multitude" or to the Romans, a unit of 3,000 - 6,000 soldiers. It's not a far stretch to say that the darkness in his life spans multiple levels. Look back at his statement to Jesus when he ran to Christ. There's something I see in this piece of dialogue. I don't think the demon is the only one doing the talking. I would argue that his humanity speaks out, too. The demons in him question why Jesus is interfering knowing full well that they have plans. Meanwhile, the human part of him speaks out, "*Are you coming to add to my pain? Don't torture me. I'm in enough pain.*"

In this story, we already see glimpses of the humanity of this tormented man verbally crying out and cutting himself. He is doing all he can to feel human again through the numbness and despair. Viewing the scene through a new lens, it makes me look at the words this man speaks to Jesus in a different light. What if both the demon and the human were interacting with Jesus? What if the human side pushed through the oppression, not wanting to be hurt by yet another human?

I love the compassion of Christ in this story. Jesus doesn't send him "thoughts and prayers." He becomes fully present with this troubled individual and restores his life. Jesus sends out the darkness, giving the man relief and freedom. He's granted this lost soul a sound mind and heart.

I think if I had been healed in that manner, I'd be running home to find my family to show them I was well. If it were me, I think I'd run back to my hometown. These would have been the same people who tried to shackle me up in the tombs. They would have needed to hear about the healing Jesus gave me. But he didn't do any of that. The man sat there. He didn't move. The Gospel of Luke tells us he approached Jesus completely unclothed. He bore nothing to reveal his identity. He owned nothing to cover himself with. He had been an outcast to the community. Yet, Jesus took notice of him, interacted with him, and helped usher in a new season of freedom for the man.

Why didn't he immediately run home? Simply put, he was a "battery chicken." The cage of darkness was taken away, yet there was something in his brain that locked him in, telling him that he wasn't free. In fact, the Scripture continues, to tell us about when the people of the nearby city came to find him *"sitting at the feet of Jesus, clothed and in his right mind." (Mark 5:35 NLT)*. He hadn't moved. Enough time elapsed for people to run back to the city, spread the news, then come back with a crowd to see what had happened. All that time took place, he was set free, but he didn't move.

So it is with those of us living in depression. We have moments where the cloud lifts, yet our attitude, mindset, and even focus remains locked in a depressive mode. We feel stuck, wondering if or when "our old self" will return. We don't want to allow hope to return, only to be let down when the shadows creep back in. I mean, IYKYK.

To those reading who have never dealt with depression: We DO want hope. We DO want healing. We DO want the things we hear the church sing and preach about. What we are nervous about is others adding to our pain. Like the man in our story who said, *"Are you coming to add to my pain? Don't torture me. I'm in enough pain."*, we're concerned that others are going to heap more burdens upon us to add to what we are already dealing with.

Give us hope and not judgment. We already judge ourselves.

Give us authentic friendship. We need more than a token handshake and small talk.

Give us listening ears, before rushing to offer advice.

Give us space to hurt, without pushing us through a "process" that makes you feel more comfortable.

Give us room to be human without over-spiritualizing things. Forced spiritual cliches and platitudes can make us feel even more disconnected from God and our faith community. Show us *your* humanity rather before you "preach" ideals.

Remind us that our mustard-sized faith is just as powerful as your faith.

Don't tell us you'll pray for us later. Offer prayer to us right then and there.

When you see a turnaround in our lives, don't expect our response to be what you think it *should* be.

Be patient with us.

Protect us; surround us in our vulnerability ("nakedness"). Clothe us with encouragement and authentic friendship.

If we don't move or act immediately, in the way you expected, it could be that we're simply "battery chickens." We might not be operating in a healthy way because, well, we just don't know how.

We will need counseling. We will need family (both relatives and church). We will need accountability and connection. We're going to need mentoring and coaching. It's going to take us some time and a lot of support to realize we are no longer caged. We're going to need patience from people as we learn about our new freedoms and to develop new, holistic, healthy routines and lifestyles. Will it happen over night? Nope. But once we are let out of our cage, with the proper environment, we can learn to be free.

All of this for me?

The final part of the story deeply touches my heart. Even as I type this, tears are pouring down my face.

As Jesus was getting into the boat, the man who had been demon-possessed begged to go with him. But Jesus said, "No, go home to your family, and tell them everything the Lord has done for you and how merciful he has been." So the man started off to visit the Ten Towns of that region and began to proclaim the great things Jesus had done for him; and everyone was amazed at what he told them.

Mark 5:18-20 NLT

This man encountered Jesus and didn't want to leave him. After reading this story, I can totally relate to his reluctance to part ways. When you are dealing with depression and you find something or someone life-giving, you latch on and you don't want to let go. This is why I refuse to abandon my faith regardless of the actions of some church leaders, denominations, and/or individual Christians. My faith must not be in others, or things, but in Christ alone. He's my hope. He is my life-source.

Look at the first verse of Luke 5,

So they arrived at the other side of the lake, in the region of the Gerasenes.

Mark 5:1 NLT

Then look at verse 21 at the end of the story,

Jesus got into the boat again and went back to the other side of the lake...

Mark 5:21 NLT

Jesus' sole purpose for this stop on this shore of the Sea of Galilee was to set one person free. Someone's inner darkness, their depth of despair, was so important to Jesus that before he headed off to speak to a crowd, he spoke to one troubled man. On this side of heaven, we don't know his name. I find encouragement in this little detail. As nameless and faceless my depression makes me feel, this part of the story encourages me to know that my importance doesn't hinge on other people's assessment of my life but on God's appraisal of me.

This nameless man was important because Jesus saw him as important.

YOU are important because Jesus sees you as important.

You don't have to live numb to life; unconscious yet conscious.

There's more to this life than just existing. You can have the same hope and freedom today that this man in the story received.

First, do what our friend did: run to Jesus. He came to Jesus with nothing to offer but himself. He was naked. Most likely, he was scarred from being bound up by the local community who didn't know what else to do with him. The human side of him was tired of the pain and desperate for relief. In our culture, we are good at dressing up for church. The goal isn't to dress up for Jesus as much as we are covering up our messy lives to fool the people we sit next to in the pew. With Jesus, you can approach him "as is." No masks. No covering. Just vulnerable with all of your scars. And the beautiful thing is that He won't turn you away.

You may be thinking, *"But Dave, I'm not feeling loved nor accepted by God. I'm numb to any type of emotional connection."* This is where I repeat what I've said in other chapters: Truth trumps feelings. When the Scripture says, *"Anyone who calls upon the Lord WILL be saved." (Romans 10:13 NLT *emphasis mine)*, that can be taken as truth. So when you don't feel lovable, acceptable, or if you don't feel anything at all, it doesn't negate the grace of God towards you and God's availability to give you healing and freedom. It doesn't matter if you feel naked and vulnerable. You are loved. In Christ, you are accepted by God. That is truth!

Second, talk it out. I love the bluntness of this man. "Don't torture me; don't add to my pain?" His humanity cried out to the only person who was willing to listen. How do I know that? We're told that the community around him (which would include his family, friends, and neighbors) banished him to the nearby cemetery and tried to chain him here. In this culture, you didn't move away when you came to adulthood. You stayed in the neighborhood you grew up in to begin your family. The rejection he went through was on a deep level. The only solution the people closest to him offered, left him scarred from the ropes and chains. He was scarred physically and emotionally from being isolated, living in the tombs.

When this man approached Jesus, he wasn't told to be quiet. He was asked questions. Jesus let the man speak. And upon him being set free, this man was found, *"...sitting there fully clothed and perfectly sane..." (Mark 5:16 NLT)* I can imagine the questions he had for

Jesus and the stories he was sharing from his life and upbringing. When the people that had bound his hands and feet showed up, they found he was not only physically unbound, but his soul had been unbound as well.

This man had a new start. His first response was to leave the people who left him. Jesus' remark to him was not to do what others inflicted upon him. *"No, go home to your family, and tell them everything the Lord has done for you and how merciful he has been." (Mark 5:19 NLT)* Jesus knew that there was more healing that needed to be done. Just because the mind and soul found healing in the moment, there was a litany of history with the community that needed healing.

Go talk about it. Like a battery chicken, you may think you are still bound by your depression, and you can't talk about what you've gone through (or are still going through). Talk about it. Get a Christ-centered counselor. Get a pastor who'll listen. Sit with your spouse. Have a conversation with your kids. Don't allow the darkness to make you suffer in silence feeling like no one will understand. Let's be real. Will everyone understand? Nope. Some will. Others will take some time. Take the advice from Jesus and go back to those that don't get it and show the patience they should have shown you. Give the grace you expected to get. Tell them about what the shadows are like. Most importantly, tell them about the freedom you now have in Christ.

It's time to stretch your wings. In Christ, you are no longer caged, unable to move beyond what the darkness has confined you to. I get the numb feelings. I get the idea behind pulling away because you can't feel anything anymore.

Truth trumps feelings.

You ARE loved by God.

You ARE needed by people around you.

You ARE valued in this world.

You may not *feel* that way. It doesn't take away from the fact that all three of those statements are truth. If you KNOW, then you WILL KNOW.

Survival Tips for the Shadows:
The healthier I am, the healthier my mental and emotional self is.

Everything within us is intrinsically connected. Our physical, mental, emotional, and spiritual components are intrinsically linked together. Good or bad, whatever happens to one part affects the other.

During the 2020 Olympics, gymnast Simone Biles withdrew from an event because of her mental health. She was physically able to compete, but something happened in her mental health that made her decide that she would endanger herself if she stayed in the competition. She recognized the physical and mental are not separate. They are connected.

I remember watching social media explode. Some were in support; others were criticizing her. Personally, I applaud the decision as you could not question her physical ability or her track record showed how strong of a competitor she was. She took a stand and brought the issue of mental health to the world's stage.

Consider how the four parts of us (physical, spiritual, emotional, and mental) are like tires. If one is out of balance or not aligned, it wears on the other three in an unhealthy and often unbalanced way.

When I tend to my physical, mental, and spiritual health, I have observed my depression to be less frequent and less severe. Exercising, resting, eating correctly, worshiping Christ, establishing proper boundaries, having fun, praying, cultivating healthy friendships, serving, finding solitude, and getting proper sleep all can aid in creating a healthier, more balanced individual. It's not about getting into a shape or size, but entering into an intentional mode for a healthy overall life.

Today is a good day to take inventory on your life. Is there something out of alignment spiritually? How about physically? If you work to make these areas healthier, don't be surprised when your mental and emotional well-being improve, too. What can you do to create a stronger you by strengthening other areas?

- 7 -

CRUSH DEPTH

Grander earth has quaked before
Moved by the sound of His voice
Seas that are shaken and stirred
Can be calmed and broken for my regard
And through it all, through it all
My eyes are on You
And through it all, through it all
It is well

- "It is Well" by Bethel Music

*"From the end of the earth I call to you when my heart
is faint. Lead me to the rock that is higher than I."*

Psalm 61:2 ESV

I've proudly worn the mantle of being a pastor who's always performing weddings. It's a huge honor to be asked and to participate in this amazing, precious, life event. I'm also known for the picture I take while officiating. Since I have my iPad in my hands for my wedding notes, I enjoy taking a picture of the bride as she comes down the aisle. I post it later on in Instagram saying,

"Always the best seat in the house. Congrats to _____ *and* _____ *!*

#WeddingPastor

After 25+ years of marrying couples, I've met a ton of other people who work weddings. From coordinators, to caterers, to venue managers, and photographers, I've had the great privilege of meeting and working with some amazing people. Whether or not you break the bank for a wedding DJ, you need to hire a great one. Having someone who knows how to address the crowd, transition through the elements of the day (hopefully in a non-awkward way), and then know what to play during the various stages of dancing during the reception, really sets the tone of the night. The DJ should know exactly what the "feel good songs" are. There are certain songs that make people flock to the dance floor and have a fantastic time. The right song creates a specific response, which in turn sets the atmosphere for that moment in time.

Do you have a go-to song, or songs, that make you happy? I think we all do. I know my wife loves songs that remind her of summer (to my dismay, most of those are country western). I'm pretty eclectic when it comes to music. I have quite a few songs that seem to immediately bring a smile to my face. There's something transformative about having a song move something within you, and making you want to roll the windows down in your car and blast the song for the world to hear.

Why do songs do that? I've heard that music can cause an endorphin release, similar to what runners experience as a "runners high." Endorphins are well-known as the hormones released in the brain in response to pain or stress. So, when we listen to meaningful songs, they can create a soothing experience that can help us through troubling times.

Psychologically speaking, music can do a few things to us. Researchers have found that upbeat music such as dance songs can boost a person's mood. Perhaps that's why dancing has been known to enhance mental health. The beat starts, the body moves, then moods and attitudes shift within you. Music can also trigger powerful emotions that are connected to past moments in your life. That's why the feelings that are most common to music are joy, strength, and relaxation. In essence, happy songs literally help create happiness.

On the subject of "happy songs," I've asked myself who is the "happiest band" of all time? What band comes to mind? For me, it's The Beach Boys. In my first job as a teenager, I worked at the Dollar Tree for a whopping $3.15 an hour. The only radio station we were allowed to play was what we called the "Oldies station." Instead of playing classics from the '50's and '60's, it seemed the station was all about The Beach Boys, occasionally throwing in a few songs by other bands. Needless to say, I got burned out on Oldies music for a time. Then the next summer rolls around and listening to The Beach Boys is, once again, a necessary part of summertime. It's hard to ignore their sound and the feelings they invoke.

For generations, Americans could identify their popular hits, some including

"Good Vibrations"

"California Girls"

"Surfin USA"

"I get around"

"Fun, fun, fun"

These songs were meant to make us daydream about flying out to California and taking surfing lessons. Some people have never visited the west coast, but they know what to expect. Why? They listened to The Beach Boys. Regardless of your location or the time of the year, their music could consistently transport you to summers on the Pacific Ocean. The Beach Boys had this effect on generations of listeners.

Would it shock you to know that the co-founder of The Beach Boys, the man who wrote those five songs I listed (and almost 200 more), a man responsible for giving us some of the happiest songs in history, was riddled by the weight of depression? He is referred to as a musical genius. He has been called one of the most innovative and significant songwriters of the 20th century. He's a Grammy winner and in the Rock & Roll Hall of Fame. Yet behind the abilities and the accolades was a man struggling.

His name is Brian Wilson. Brian knew life in the shadows all too well.

In just five years after the debut of their first album (1962, Surfin' Safari), they had risen to international stardom. Their sound could be recognized around the world. However in 1967, Brian would suffer an emotional breakdown. The pressure to be on stage made him uncomfortable and he began to withdraw from social interactions with the group. He sunk deeper and deeper into a life of drugs. Alcohol began to control his life. Instead of being out in front leading the band, he retreated to play a role behind the scenes. As The Beach Boys continued to flourish, Brian's life continued to spiral. His substance abuse grew to the point that he was so dependent, he thought he couldn't stop the behaviors. It wasn't till the mid-'70s when he would finally get help and regain forward momentum.

A songwriter and performer of the "happiest band," singing the "happiest songs," was actually the most unhappy human being. Overshadowed by his inner turmoil, Brian was broken by the pressure of who he was supposed to be. Everyone expected him to "be" someone, to fill a leadership role and create and perform amazing, uplifting, lighthearted music. The pressure became too much and he left the iconic band he helped elevate.

If there's anything that I can take from his story (and I can pull several lessons) it is simply this: Pressure by itself can be debilitating. If you deal with depression, pressure can be lethal. Navigating pressure while trying to work though the shadows can be a lethal combination that can easily overwhelm any human being. So, before we talk more about depression, let's talk more about pressure. Why? Every single one of us has a "crush depth."

Crush Depth

"Pressure" can be described as a continuous force applied to an object. It's not something foreign to any one of us. We all experience pressure in every second of life. We may not always perceive it, but the earth's atmosphere is constantly putting pressure on us. Have you ever heard a meteorologist talk about air pressure? Earthly air presses down on us at a rate of 14.5 pounds per square inch. Since our bodies are used to this exact amount of atmospheric pressure, we can have physical responses to changes in it. That's why you and I may have headaches (or know someone who does) when the barometric pressure drops. If you change the pressure around us, our bodies will be quick to notice.

Not only do we experience external pressure, but our insides are under pressure, too. There is a healthy force that our blood should be flowing under (normal blood pressure is roughly 120/80). That's why when visiting the doctor, one of the first things they'll check is our blood pressure. It's a great indicator of malfunction in the body, very similar to the indicator lights on the dashboard of a car. Have you ever gone flying and had discomfort in your ears? When you leave the ground, your internal pressure is no longer equal to the ambient Earth-surface pressure, and you feel the difference in your ears. Our bodies have several air-filled spaces including the lungs, stomach, sinuses, and ears, that each have their own pressure which must be maintained. When something from the outside (altitude of airplane) changes the pressure on the inside (of our ears for example), we can experience it physically (ear popping or discomfort during takeoff and landing).

Another example is if we dive into water and go down to certain depths, we can feel pressure building in our ears and in our lungs. I love snorkeling. Did you know that for every 33 feet of water you swim downward, the pressure increases on your body by 15 pounds per square inch? The deeper we go, the more your body must try to adapt to the increased water pressure. If you were to dive 100 feet deep without any gear, your body goes into what's called a "dive response." It's the body's reaction to help you survive. In a dive response, your body responds by pushing your oxygenated blood towards the heart and brain tissues, pulling the oxygenated blood away from everything else.

You might not realize that in the ocean, it's not a lack of oxygen that can become harmful, halt exploration, or prevent discovery. It's the pressure from the weight of the water. I know what you're thinking, "*what about submarines?*" As well-built as they are, subs still have limits that keep most of the ocean floor protected from human exploration. Submarines have what's called a "collapse depth," perhaps more commonly known as their "crush depth." The crush depth is the water depth at which a vessel implodes due to the pressure of the water. Wrap your head around this: even with all the technology we possess in our modern time, the pressure in the depths of the oceans keep more than 80% of the deep waters unmapped, unobserved, and unexplored. The brightest minds and the most able hands cannot overcome the strongest pressures of the oceans. This tells me that even our best-built watercraft, the latest and greatest of our marine designs and innovations, have their limits. They all have a "crush depth," none of which extend adequately to reach the goal of our ocean floors.

We cannot talk about depression and not talk about pressure. Pressure gets the best of us. I've seen athletes break under pressure at the highest levels. From the Olympics to the Super Bowl, if someone doesn't perform on the grandest stage, words like "choke" and "crack" are used to describe their performance under pressure. It's a label that hangs around their neck unless they can hoist a championship trophy and rid themselves of their failure. The Buffalo Bills are not known as a dominant team by reaching four Super Bowls in a row. Instead, they are known as the team that lost four straight championships. In the 1996 Masters, Greg Norman set a course record in his opening round. Going into the final round with a 6-stroke lead, Greg lost by 5 strokes. He's not known for amassing 89 professional wins, rather, he is known for his collapses to the pressure in the Masters Tournament. One that's close to my heart, the 1993 NCAA Basketball National Championship, my Michigan Wolverines were attempting to beat North Carolina. In the closing seconds, Chris Webber attempted to call a timeout when his team didn't have any, which cost his team a foul, possession of the ball, and ultimately the game. Never mind that he and four of his other teammates (i.e., the Fab Five) just led their team to the National Championship 2 years in a row as teenagers. Instead, a moment of cracking under pressure follows his legacy in college basketball.

I share these examples to prove a point: pressure can get to all of us. There is not a single person out there who is immune to pressure. It's everywhere. You can't escape it. Pressure has existed since the beginning of time. If you wanted food, you had the pressure of hunting, gathering, or harvesting it. That means if you did not plant well, have luck gathering, or constantly hunt for your catch, then you and your family did not eat.

That's pressure.

I Feel < (Lesser Than)

Pressure follows us wherever we go. We have it at work. It's waiting for us at home. You feel it at church. The holidays are filled with it. It shows up at birthdays. Whether it is all-encompassing or seemingly minuscule, pressure is present in practically everything we engage in.

Do you get stressed out by traffic? There is the pressure of feeling confined by traffic laws and the presence of other cars, laced with the urgency of being on time to your destination. Can you remember taking an exam in a quiet classroom, trying to concentrate through the sound of the clock ticking? You may recall the pressure of remembering everything you studied, the weight of people's expectations, and the sound of people setting their pencils down because they finished before you. Just typing that out stresses me and I haven't been in school for over twenty years. As you can see, pressure is present even in the monotony of life.

To add to the normal pressures of life, attached to our hands or in our back pockets is a cell phone that makes us accessible at all times.

On those phones, we have social media apps to help us keep track of the goings-on of everyone in our lives, as well as world news from a variety of platforms. As a result, we see what others are doing, which makes us feel obligated to post thoughts and pictures to keep up with them. If you turn on the news, you are bombarded with reports of what's wrong and who's to blame. (I mean, when was the last time you turned on national news to hear what was going right in our world?) Constant access, a continuous feed of what people are up to, and around-the-clock information are enough to break even the strongest amongst us.

Working with teenagers as a youth pastor for 12 years, in addition to raising my now adult children, I've had to navigate this "<" (lesser than) feeling when it comes to students dealing with the expectations of their parents. Parents become frustrated with their children because, "*When I was a teenager, I was able to do* _____." I'd have to remind the parent, "*Just because you share DNA, it doesn't mean your child is exactly like you.*" Sounds elementary doesn't it? Yet, if we're not careful as parents, we can place unfair expectations based on our own personalities and abilities, not realizing that our kids may not be like us at all. Please hear my heart: I *want* you to have expectations for your kids. It's okay to challenge them. It's okay to have healthy expectations for your children. That said, be cautious to curb what you *expect* with the *reality* of how God created your child. I wonder how many of our kids are made to feel "<" because simply they don't measure up to what we did at their age and/or do now.

Some people may *seem* to navigate levels of pressure better than others. Certain temperaments and personalities can steer pressure-filled situations better than others, simply by their nature. I think I may be one of those people. I'm one who can work (temporarily, at least) under the weight of a short timeframe with big expectations. It's a gift that I believe I get through my mother. She served as the pastor's secretary in a large church for over 30 years. She's a rockstar at being able to work with short turnarounds under a lot of pressure. Our pastor would work on his message until Sunday morning service was starting. He would hand my mom his notes for her to prepare slides minutes before entering the pulpit. This wasn't an odd moment but a weekly occurrence. This is how she worked every single Sunday.

I recall her heading out on vacation, so her Sunday morning task was assigned to another administrative assistant. I thought I should check in on her replacement, only to find her in tears. The pressure of getting the information last minute and translating it to the projection slides had already overwhelmed her. I felt comfortable doing the task myself, so I sent her into service and took over the task.

I want to make a statement about this amazing coworker of mine: She wasn't "<" me. She wasn't less talented than me, nor was I a better employee than her. She wasn't bad at her job. In fact, she thrived at the office and was well loved. That said, in that particular circumstance, the challenge the pressure presented was just too much for her personality type at that moment. Maybe it was the day or the week she had. Perhaps it was the situation in general. We as humans have the proclivity to live in comparison to others, which in turn can cause us to see ourselves as "<", as inferior or less capable. *"If I can't do what others can do, I must not be as good as them."*

I thrive completing tasks under pressure. The nice thing about tasks is that there is a beginning and an end. That works for me. Early in adulthood, pressures that linger caused me to struggle much more than specific tasks with a tight turnaround. Pressures with no specific box to check; the ones I couldn't get away from, really gnawed at me. Pastoral ministry isn't a 9-5 job. I'm Pastor Dave in people's eyes 24/7. Though I had office hours, I didn't know how to shut my mind off of "pastor mode", nor how to get out of the pressures it brought. I couldn't turn it off. After a few years of this non-stop need to perform, the pressure broke me.

Looking back, the beginning of my pastoral ministry was the season of life where I really experienced some of the darkest depths of my shadows. I didn't know at the time what I was battling against. Nobody talked about depression, especially not in the church. I didn't have any coping mechanisms, and in my mind, counseling wasn't an option. I didn't know what to tell Anne. I didn't know what to tell my parents, who, at the time, were on staff with me. I didn't know any other minister who dealt with depression because, again, we as pastors historically don't feel we can discuss it with each other. I felt alone and I felt like an outcast. I'd see other ministers in my position, whose churches or responsibilities were smaller in size, with less of a portfolio than I possessed, yet they appeared to be thriving under the pressures of their jobs. Some of those pastors even had to work additional jobs outside of the church to support their families and they still *seemed* healthier than me.

The pressure got to me. Since I didn't know anything about depression at the time, the pressure was compounded by the darkness whispering this one thought into my ear:

"I AM < EVERYONE."

Ladies and gentlemen, this could not be further from the truth. No matter who you are. The "greatness" of your life is not found in comparison to others, rather in what God sees in you and what He has placed in you. *You are "fearfully and wonderfully made" (Psalm 139:14 NIV).* You are gifted by Him. You are necessary in this world. You are NEVER alone, as God is with you in EVERY step of life. He doesn't toss us away at the slightest hint of a mistake. His grace covers us. This idea of < vs. > is not what God has called us to live but what we've come up with in our humanity, to measure ourselves. Stop creating metrics to show your superiority over (or inferiority under) others, and humbly see your uniqueness that is sovereignly given by God.

You are not "<". Your depression may make you feel "<". The pressure can make you perceive that you are "<". Grasp onto the truth.

In Christ, you are,

- > (greater than) the darkness.
- > the pain.
- > the struggles.
- > voices that tell you, "You are not enough."

The pressure will push you to live from a place of "<".

My encouragement to you: Be ">". Rise above. Live from that place. See your life as ">", not because of what you can do (your ability) but because of what Christ has done and what He is going to do through you (who you are). Find your footing in Christ's presence and His power working in your life. The pressure of our lives, culture, jobs, etc. can make you see life differently than you were intended to.

Pressure will fool you into thinking that your strength comes from you and not from the Lord. Fight against that and live a life of ">".

Like a Frog in a Pot

In the Scriptures, the book of Judges is given a name that many misunderstand. Israel used a particular type of leader to rule the nation prior to their kings. They had what would eventually be called "judges." Get Judge Judy and other magistrates out of your head. We're not talking about someone who leads a courtroom, but regional political leaders. You can compare them to a tribal leader of sorts or a governor over a territory.

Of the biblical judges in Israel, there may be none more notable than Samson. Simply using his name brings up all sorts of images and stories. Known as the "strongest man" of his time, his exploits included feats and accomplishments that could only be achieved by someone with immense strength and ability. From reading Scripture, we know that his diet or a workout routine was not the source of his strength. He became strong when the *Spirit of the Lord came powerfully upon him" (Judges 14:6 NLT)*. While we may picture Samson with a bodybuilder physique, many have claimed that Samson may have actually had a more *normal* body type, illustrating that his abilities couldn't be attributed to what he could develop on his own but a strength that only came from the Lord.

I love that Scripture shares stories of real people. It shows us human beings as they are without covering up the messiness of their lives. We get to see both faults and successes; we see their highs and lows. I find encouragement in that despite all my faults and failings, God can still work in and through someone like me. It gives me courage to share what I perceive as my personal flaws with others, that we may better understand and encourage one another instead of a life of continued comparison. Here in the book of Judges, Samson is a man of authority and power. He's a man of great reputation and he is well-renowned. In terms of emphasizing his humanity, the Bible doesn't hold back in revealing his imperfections.

This was a man of tremendous accomplishments. This was a man whose name brought stories of great exploits. This was a man whose presence struck fear into the hearts of his enemies. This was a man of colossal abilities. This was a man whose birth and purpose was foretold by an angel to his parents. Samson, a man so physically strong he broke off a city gate and carried it upon his shoulders *(Judges 16)*, still found himself so emotionally susceptible that he was inwardly broken by his own struggles. One of the areas he struggled with the most was the area of "pressure."

During a season of his life when he was very vulnerable to pressure, Samson fell in love with a woman, Delilah. The Lords of the Philistines, who were enemies of Samson, each paid Delilah 1,100 pieces of silver to discover and share the source of his strength in order to capture him. To grasp how much she was given, *Judges 3:3 NLT* says there were five lords of the Philistines. If each of them gave 1,100 pieces of silver, that means Delilah received 5,500 silver pieces. *Judges 17:10 NLT* tells us that 10 pieces of silver were worth a year's wage, so, in essence, Delilah is offered 550 years worth of wages for her act of betrayal. To give a modern perspective, back in 2019, the average American made just over $31,000 a year. Multiply that by what Delilah was offered and you've got a bit more than $17 million. This is the price she put on her relationship. These Lords ensured to make her an offer she couldn't refuse. Delilah would take the money and leave Samson in the hands of the Philistines.

> *So Delilah said to Samson, "Please tell me what makes you so strong and what it would take to tie you up securely."*
>
> Judges 16:6 NLT

Blinded by his heart, Samson doesn't seem to read into his lover's questions. Instead, he sends her off the trail by giving her the wrong information.

Samson replied,

> *"If I were tied up with seven new bowstrings that have not yet been dried, I would become as weak as anyone else."*
>
> Judges 16:7 NLT

After reporting this information, Delilah is brought bowstrings by the Philistine leaders. They waited for their opportunity. She bound him up. Then the Philistine men came into the room, and she screamed out,

> *"Samson! The Philistines have come to capture you!"*
>
> Judges 16:9 NLT

Surprising Delilah, Samson easily came to his feet, flexing to snap the bowstrings and then dispose of his enemies.

> *Afterward Delilah said to him, "You've been making fun of me and telling me lies!*
> *Now please tell me how you can be tied up securely."*
>
> Judges 16:10 NLT

Samson does what he did before. He gave her a fabricated answer, she bound him up, people came to capture him, he broke free, and he dealt with his enemies. If this wasn't bad enough, a THIRD time, Delilah inquires of him about the secret of his strength.

> *"You've been making fun of me and telling me lies! Now tell me how you can be tied up securely."*
>
> Judges 16:13 NLT

I bet you're thinking what I'm thinking, *"Samson, how in the world are you NOT reading into this? She's setting you up over and over!"* We have to remember that Samson was a human just like you and me. His emotions were caught up in their relationship. Delilah was trying to pressure him into telling her his secret. He was probably thinking to himself, *"I've got all of this under control."* Then for a fourth time, she pours it on. I like how the Amplified Bible says it:

> *Then she said to him, "How can you say, 'I love you,' when your heart is not with me? You have mocked me these three times and have not told me where your great strength lies." When she pressured him day after day with her words and pleaded with him, he was annoyed to death.*
>
> Judges 16:15-16 AMP

Notice the specific words, *"she pressured him day after day with her words and pleaded with him, he was annoyed to death."* We have what seemed to Samson a playful progression that has turned into pressure. He was blinded by his emotions, and he couldn't see that there was nothing "playful" about this situation. The pressure had turned from a casual request to a constant plea where he was worn down by it *"day after day."*

What Delilah didn't know is that Samson was a Nazirite. He understood that his strength came from his consecration (separation and dedication) to the Lord as a Nazirite. To give you some context, Nazirites are a people who voluntarily dedicate themselves to God. In that dedication, they prepare and live out guidelines to what they can and cannot do for a set timeframe as a part of their dedication to God. This is helpful to know as we see in *Judges 13*, his mother was told by an angel, *"his hair must never be cut."* *"For he will be dedicated to God as a Nazirite from birth."* *(Judges 13:5 NLT)* His lack of haircuts wasn't about style; it was a sign that his life was to be set apart for God's purposes. This is why verse 17 is so significant:

Finally, Samson shared his secret with her. "My hair has never been cut," he confessed, "for I was dedicated to God as a Nazirite from birth. If my head were shaved, my strength would leave me, and I would become as weak as anyone else."

Judges 16:17 NLT

Samson was so emotionally invested into the situation that he couldn't think straight. He didn't see the progression the impact the pressure was having on him. There's an old story that says if you put a frog into boiling water, he'll jump out. However, if you put a frog into a pot with room temperature water and slowly bring it to a boil, it will not jump out because it will start to tolerate the increased heat, at least until the rising temperature kills it. This is Samson. His emotions have blinded his critical thinking ability. The increased pressure wore him down day by day until he confessed his secret, positioning him perfectly for his enemies to strike.

Delilah next lulled him to sleep, cut off his hair, and the Philistines came in to capture him. What comes next is, in my opinion, one of the saddest passages in the entirety of the Bible:

…When he woke up, he thought, "I will do as before and shake myself free." But he didn't realize the Lord had left him.

Judges 16:20 NLT

One thing we should note is the wording here from Judges 16:20. The Lord didn't leave Sampson *alone*. That's impossible, as we are never apart from His presence. What this *did* mean is God's anointing (special empowerment of God) of strength on had left. He was vulnerable not just to attack, but he was also more susceptible to being captured.

Though pressure doesn't necessarily *cause* depression, it can be a catalyst that lowers your defenses. Unchecked pressure can open your heart and your mind to attack. This is exactly what we see in Samson. With all the pressure being applied to him, Samson gave into his emotions and confessed what had kept him strong. The feelings that were driving him, compounded with the pressure he was underneath, became a volatile construct that changed his life forever.

He thought to himself, "*I'll just keep going on as if nothing happened. I can still act the part. I can still function the same.*" Yet he got up and nothing was "normal." He was shaved. He was weak.

And next, he was captured.

Even the Strongest have a "Crush Depth"

The graphicness of the Scripture here paints a humiliating picture. The Philistines gouged out his eyes and made him push a mill to grind grain, yoked like an ox. This man of great fame is now relegated to do what a simple farm animal is used for.

Welcome to what depression does:

It takes your strength. "I can't do what I used to do."

It makes you feel abandoned. "God has forgotten me."

It makes you feel alone. "Even my friends and family want nothing to do with me."

It wants to humiliate you. "I am nothing close to what I used to/ should be."

It steals your sight of what reality really looks like. "Darkness is all I can see."

Samson had hit his "crush depth" leaving the champion stuck, grinding grain like an animal. His daily activity consisted of walking blindly in circles around a mill, replaying his life's choices over and over, stuck in the anguish of imagining what life *could* look like if *that moment* didn't happen. His "crush depth" came in the form of a toxic relationship. For me, my "crush depth" comes in the form of other peoples' expectations combined with my desire to work for the approval of others. For you, it may be different. What crushes you may not affect me. What pulverizes me may not even register to you as any type of duress. Perhaps your "crush depth" comes in the form of pressure that derives from some or several of these areas:

- Family obligations.
- Lack of boundaries in relationships.
- School and/or job expectations.
- Keeping up with others (competition and comparison).
- A drive to climb the leadership ladder at all costs.
- Living limitless with your schedule.
- Refusal to take proper care of yourself.

Please don't misunderstand me. There's pressure in every aspect of life that can stem from any or all of these areas. You're not going to get away from that. It's idealistic and often unrealistic to think that you can have a pressure-free life. It is always present, even if in minute forms. What can happen, if we don't recognize areas that affect us more, personally, is the tendency not to navigate that pressure in a positive, healthy way. As strong as Samson was, he didn't pay attention to where the pressure was coming from. He also failed to see how being distracted by his emotions led toward his crash into a broken reality; a reality that has materialized into a darkness he can't see past. He was in a place he thought he'd never get out of.

These are the lies of the darkness. This is what the shadows whisper. Despite this, I've got good news for you: what has crushed you previously doesn't have to have the final word. Depression may have left you feeling like you've lost it all, but God hasn't abandoned you. He didn't abandon Samson. There in the prison, Samson's hair started to grow again.

Stubble means something

> *But before long, his hair began to grow back.*
> Judges 16:22 NLT

I remind you: his hair didn't possess any magical ability. It's not like little by little, the more it grew back, the more his strength returned. I believe that as his bald head started to grow hair again, it reminded Samson of the reality that God never actually left him. It brought him back to the reason why he was born and why God set him apart.

When you are going through depression, sometimes you can't find a huge "win" or something "monumental" to celebrate. Sometimes you just need to search for the "stubble." Look for the small moments to celebrate and let that build up momentum. Things like:

• The sun is shining.

• A good moment happened at work.

• A song made you think beyond the shadows.

• A good memory came to mind.

• Somebody made you smile.

• You had a good meal.

• Nothing bad happened.

These are "stubble" moments. These are small, tiny moments when you can begin to see that a new season is on the horizon and hope is returning. That small scripture in *Judges 16:22* gives five simple realities to Samson that I want to give to you when life is crushing you.

First, God sees you. You have not fallen from His sight. Even though Samson was crushed and hidden from man's eyes in a prison, he was never out of God's sight. Second, God knows everything about your story. He knows the good, the bad, and the ugly. Not

only does He know you, God still chooses to draw close to you out
of His love for you. Third, God is always working in and on your
story. Samson couldn't see it. Sometimes we can't detect what God is
up to or even if He cares. Know this: He is working. When we can't
see God working in the foreground, it just means He is busy working
in the background. Fourth, God is greater. Period. I know what the
darkness whispers into your soul. Recognize that God's ability to
bring you out is greater than the darkness that wants to keep you
there. Lastly, God can use your present pain in your future story both
for your good and His glory. The story the shadows are trying to write
is but a chapter, merely a season. God is the author of our story. Just
because depression says "it's over" doesn't mean that God's story for
and involvement in your life is over. I say this often: like Samson, the
best has yet to come for you.

To finish the story of this fallen warrior, you only need to look
a few verses further. A drunk crowd of Philistines wants to bring
Samson out to mock him and, indirectly, mock God. As Samson is
led out, he asks to be able to rest on the main beams of the building.
There, Samson prayed a simple prayer.

*"Sovereign Lord, remember me again. O God, please strengthen me just
one more time. With one blow let me pay back the Philistines for the loss
of my two eyes."*

Judges 16:28 NLT

With his hands on the pillars, he pushed the load-bearing pillars
over, bringing the entire building down, giving him the greatest
victory over the Philistines than he had ever had before. The Scripture
tells us that this moment was a greater accomplishment than any
other time. I want to speak a last Scripture over you that I think is
important for this chapter.

*"Yet I am confident I will see the LORD's goodness while I am here in
the land of the living."*

Psalm 27:13 NLT

Don't count yourself out and think that life is over or that this
world is better without you. Don't focus upon what you lost but

appreciate what you have left. God's not done with you. He wants to do more in you and through you.

I pray Psalm 27:13 over you; that you will become confident that you WILL see the Lord's goodness, today. If not today, then tomorrow. If not tomorrow, then the next day. My point is this:

Better days are ahead.

You may have hit your "crush depth." You may feel like a shell of your old self. I want you to keep reminding yourself:

1. God sees you.

2. God knows everything about your story.

3. God is always working in and on your story.

4. God is greater. Period.

5. God can use your present pain in your future story for your good and His glory.

Survival Tips for the Shadows:
Borrowed Songs for Painful Seasons

Do you have a song that "does it" for you? A song that sends you to a place of deep meaning or specific memory. Maybe it's a song that brings good tears. Perhaps it's a song that creates a flood of memories. It might be a song that makes you feel excitement or anticipation. When I talk about songs like that, the first song that comes to mind is called "Eye of the Tiger" by Survivor. There's something about the beginning that makes me work out a little harder, run a little faster, or want to go out and box someone. I mean, that's the song Apollo Creed used on Rocky to get pumped up to fight Clubber Lang in the movie *Rocky III*. When I needed a boost in my workouts as a teenager, I'd borrow a song from Apollo's workout playlist and get myself in a mentality of "*getting strong*" (okay, I'm done with the Rocky references).

I think a great tip to navigate depression is creating a playlist of songs that recenter your heart and get down into your soul. I call them, "Borrowed Songs for Painful Seasons." You can do this in two ways. First, create a playlist on your favorite music provider (iTunes, Spotify, YouTube, etc.). Use songs that are meaningful to you, songs that bring life. As you've noticed, in each chapter, I begin with lyrics to worship songs that have been important to me during my times of depression. I want you to use songs that put words to not just your pain but also our salvation. These are songs I sing with. I cry with them. I think deeply about them. They touch my soul and bring life to me.

Second, make a "playlist" of Psalms to read. In the Scriptures, the Psalms are literal songs and poems written during pivotal life moments. Some are written by David. Others are penned by people connected to him. Psalms 42 and 43 are special to me (and tattooed to my wrist). Psalms 23, 61, 91, and 121 are special, too. Read the Psalms and make your playlist from ones which minister to your soul.

If you can't write your own songs, borrow them from others. The authors won't mind, and the lyrics can help breathe life back into you.

- 8 -

I HATE WHAT I SEE

When I doubt it, Lord, remind me
I'm wonderfully made
You're an artist and a potter
I'm the canvas and the clay

- "It is Well" by Bethel Music

"Save me and rescue me, for you do what is right. Turn your ear to listen to me, and set me free."

Psalm 71:2 NLT

Do you recognize the line, "*Magic mirror on the wall, who's the fairest one of all?*" (Often misquoted as "*Mirror Mirror on the wall...*") It's from the classic 1937 Disney film, "*Snow White and the Seven Dwarfs.*" This film is legendary as it was the first feature-length animated film in U.S. history. Based on a German fairytale, this movie was so unique to the industry that when the Academy of Motion Picture Arts and Sciences gave out their annual awards, Disney was given a special Oscar with seven mini-Oscars, as this movie had no category because one did not yet exist. Like I said, this was a pioneer film; truly, a groundbreaking project.

In the film, there is the iconic scene of the character we know as the Evil Queen who looks into a magical mirror daily to validate her beauty, dreading any signs of aging and illustrating her vanity. This works fine for her until the mirror informs her that there is one who is fairer than her. In a rage, she gets the mirror to tell her about Snow White, and she seeks to eliminate this young woman, to help protect her face as the "fairest in the kingdom." The Evil Queen's drive, her outlook on the world, began and ended with what she saw in the mirror every day.

I relate to this.

One of the terrible effects that depression can have on the soul is its ability to change how we interpret the image we see in the mirror. The shadows distort and manipulate how we see our reflection to the point where we see an image in the mirror nobody else would recognize but us. However, because WE see it, we then place that perspective on those in our social circles and assume they can see what we see; that they feel what we feel. This often sends us tumbling down another shadowy rabbit hole of loneliness, frustration, and self-deprecation.

I'm talking about "self-hate."

Being bullied from the inside

Every once in a while, someone will talk about how they'd love to go back to their middle school days. I think that's insane. Who in the world wants to relive the years of puberty and awkward social changes of that season of life? Not me. When I look back on those years, it was tough. It was challenging enough with what I was dealing with when it came to my body, a change of schools, and the shaping of the social side of things. Then I began to encounter something I didn't anticipate: bullying. Some of the people I grew up with in my neighborhood as friends, became my worst nightmares. Going to school wasn't so bad. I either walked or rode my bike for the 1 1/2-mile journey (although Michigan winters can make that mile and a half feel like five miles). During school my active friendships kept things light and enjoyable. Mornings were never really bad, but after school, things became unbearable.

I don't know why things after school were the way they were. I don't understand why the group I went home with changed. It could be because my friends were in different extracurricular activities. I played football and ran track. Others did clubs. Often, I found myself traveling home alone. That's where the misery began. Being chased home to be beaten up and spit on, regularly, was terrible. I've been asked why I didn't tell my parents or any authorities. Part of it was the mentality, "*snitches get stitches.*" In my brain, reporting anything was going to invite more attention from my bullies, and that meant more pain. Second, there was something mentally in me that thought if I told my mom and dad, it was going to invite, unpleasant reactions. Maybe I was going to come off as a disappointment to them (which wasn't true). Possibly they'd get mad at me for not standing up for myself (which wasn't going to happen). Perhaps they'd blame themselves for having a wimp as a son (which would never be the case). To this day, I'm embarrassed at my "embarrassment" at telling them. Ask anyone who's gone through any type of abuse, and they'll concur with some of those same mentalities.

I remember one Wednesday night at church, my friend Tim saw me holding my belly in youth group and asked me if I was alright. I wasn't. My stomach was cramping already anticipating the next day's bullying. It now had gone from this being something that affected my life after school, to carrying this physical manifestation of anxiety even outside when in a different environment. Tim was the first person I was brave enough to talk to about being bullied. He encouraged me to talk to my parents (which I didn't do), and to get some "help." Let's be real, being bullied had already done its job. It shifted my view of the world around me by transforming how I viewed myself. I was being abused by "friends," and I thought it was my fault. I couldn't tell my parents because I was ashamed of what I felt I had "allowed" to happen. If I told on them, I'd be labeled a snitch and I'd be ostracized by my remaining friends. Instead of hating the bullying, I started hating myself.

Self-hate is so similar to being bullied. The difference is you are bullying yourself from the inside. Instead of a bully waiting for you outside of school, this bully follows you around every day, criticizing you and pointing out every single flaw you possess. This bully shames you for every mistake you make. Self-hate has this way of giving yourself unhealthy doses of self-criticism that shames you into thinking that you cannot possibly deserve goodness, have good things, and/or experience any goodwill in life.

Those of us who experience self-hate in our depression often will say things to ourselves like:

- *"Why do you even try?"*
- *"What's wrong with you?"*
- *"You're the worst."*
- *"I knew you would fail."*
- *"You're a loser."*
- *"No one wants to be around you."*
- *"Of course you messed up. What did you expect?"*
- *"Can't you just be normal like everyone else?"*

I wish it wasn't this way. Life in our world shouldn't be this way.

It would be bad enough if these comments came from people in our lives, but they are particularly devastating when they come from the bully that lives within us. It's extremely frustrating to doubt every compliment or kind comment. It is exhausting to question every positive thing that happens while we are "waiting for the shoe to drop."

I can hear a few of you thinking, "*Well, don't feel that way. Don't think like that. Just stop it.*"

If it were only that easy. If depression and its effects could simply be turned on and off like a light switch, believe me, we'd do it. None of us who live with the shadows lingering over us want to talk this way, let alone, think this way. Nevertheless, we do.

"A + B + C = self-hate"

The question I get about self-hate is, "*Why would someone feel that way about themselves?*" or "*What causes people to hate themselves?*" The simplest way to answer the first question is to say, "*It's not a choice they're making as much as a response to personal pain.*" Nobody grows up wanting to despise the person they see in the mirror. No child dreams of the day when they stop loving themselves. Pain has shrouded the image they see every morning, and it has manipulated their appearance to the point the individual sees a different creature than what everyone around them sees.

The second question is a bit more complicated. What causes self-hate has an answer that is not as simple as you may want. Usually, people are trying to nail down an event or moment that their view of themselves became bleak. The reality is: it's not about one singular event. It's not even about two bad moments that create this self-loathing mentality. Truth be told, it happens over time and typically is generated by a few factors at play, both external and internal. There could be a traumatic event involved that deeply impacted a person. There could be mental pressures to perform, like perfectionism, comparison, or unmet expectations. There can be environmental factors that stem from a home life or work life that foster a learned behavior that isn't very healthy. All of that to say: There's no A + B + C = self-hate. It really depends upon the individual, what they've experienced, their physical and emotional makeup, their environment, relational health, and their perspective of life.

Life can navigate differently for everyone. That's why you can see two individuals go through the same traumatic event and see one come out seemingly unscathed while the other is in therapy for years. There's no equation that says, "*This is exactly why people are dealing with self-hate.*" I don't think I'll ever completely understand why depression happens in some and not in others. Self-hate presents itself, it can manifest itself in several ways. Perhaps you've heard a friend, or even yourself, say a few of these statements:

• My emotions are factual. "*If I feel like a failure then I must be a failure.*"

• I must strive for approval. "*My view of myself is dependent upon your appraisal (approval) of me.*"

• I reject compliments. "*That person was just being nice to me. If they really knew me, then they wouldn't have said that.*"

• I push away friendships. "*I don't know why (friend) would want to spend time with me.*"

• All criticism is personal. "*They must not like me to say that. I can't let it go.*"

• I fixate on the negative. "*I can't see the ten good moments when one bad moment has happened.*"

• My self-esteem is perpetually low. "*It's hard to see how I'm gifted when I see everyone else around me excelling.*"

• I employ "*all-in*" thinking. "*I made a mistake, so everything is ruined. I'm a failure.*"

• I purposely cut down others. "*I can't handle others succeeding so I cut them down in order to feel better about myself.*"

• I shut out positive people. "*If I allow them closer and they see the real me, they won't understand me and I'll end up hurt and even more alone.*"

• I can't have a vision for the future. "*I want success but I'm afraid to fail. Besides, whatever I try, won't have much of an impact at all.*"

• I possess cynical vision. "*Most people don't understand how the* real-world works. I do. *Regardless of what anyone tries, it will never get better.",* or even, *"I hate this world."*

• I can't forgive myself. *"I can't get past the decision (or mistake) I've made. Why try again? I'll just mess it up like I did the last time."*

• I hold pity parties. *"There's no way I can succeed in life. Nobody has the hand I've been dealt with. Life is stacked against me."*

Can you feel the self-loathing in that list? Perhaps a better question is: have you said any of those statements to yourself? Do you personally connect to a few of them? I know I have. It seems that different seasons and moments have invited a few of them.

This is a Heart Issue

Let's be real, I think most, if not all, of those reading this can say at least one or two of those remarks sound familiar and have appeared in your thoughts regarding yourself. I say this to make the point that you cannot help a thought come into your head. However, you do have a choice on whether you allow the mindset behind those thoughts to be a visitor or a resident. I hope that makes sense. Too often, when these outlooks appear in our thinking, they come to take ownership of your mind as if it's theirs to claim. I want to encourage you with this: You do not have to be a victim of every thought that comes your way. Thoughts are not truth. Feelings are not truth. You and I need a steady and sure foundation that we can stand on when everything within us is shifting. It's what the Psalmist is talking about when he writes,

"From the ends of the earth, I cry to you for help when my heart is overwhelmed. Lead me to the towering rock of safety."

Psalm 61:2 KJV

We need that steadying rock that remains as solid footing when we are overwhelmed by what's going on in our heart. Some of you reading this will be saying, *"Dave, what I'm dealing with has nothing to do with my heart; it's in my head."* Let me explain.

To understand this Scripture more deeply, you'll need an understanding of what is meant by *"heart"* from a Hebrew perspective. To the modern Western world, our heart is the seat of our emotions. That's why we say things like, "*I love you with all of my heart,*" or "*My heart sank when I heard the news.*" That said, the Psalmist here was King David, and he was writing in ancient Hebrew times. In that culture, the seat of their emotions was their "*bowels*" (intestines, innards, stomach). It came from the idea that when you feel something deeply, it comes from your gut. This could create some very interesting Valentine's cards … "*I love you with all of my bowels.*"

So why did the writer use the word "heart" and not "bowels"? Because from the perspective of his culture, the heart wasn't the seat of emotions but the seat of the mind and will. When the writer says, "*I cry to you when my heart is overwhelmed,*" to translate it to our modern culture, he is actually saying, "*I cry to you when my MIND is overwhelmed.*"

Does that change the scope of what you thought you understood about the passage? If you're familiar with Scripture, I bet you are reconsidering all the times "heart" is referred to in Scripture, as it will completely transform some of the things you've read. Psalm 61:2 helps us to see, first, that even the best of us can be overwhelmed. In other words, struggle is not exclusive to those of us who think we're the only ones who struggle. Darkness does not discriminate.

David, outside of Jesus, is one of the most well-known figures in Biblical history. In Jewish history, he is one of the most important individuals, known as their greatest king. To look upon the flag of Israel, what do you see? The star of David. So, yes, David is remembered and revered, honored and highly esteemed. This leader of leaders, this beloved king, the only person who was ever referred to as "a man after God's own heart" (1 Samuel 13:14; Acts 13:22 NLT), even this great and powerful man had moments when his mind got the best of him.

What we tend to do with Scripture is to deify the individuals we read about. We put them up on pedestals and hold them in such high regard that we think daily or practical issues couldn't touch them. Better said: we forget Biblical figures were completely human, just like us. It's important to point that out because I find that when people struggle, they think that either they are the only one to do so and/or that there's something wrong with them because, "*good or*

Godly people don't shouldn't struggle like this."

Now enters King David.

This is the man who wrote at least 73 of the 150 Psalms, admits openly to you and me that he gets overwhelmed by his thoughts. This monarch, this man hand picked by God to lead, experiences what us average individuals experience: being flooded by thoughts that want to drown us in negativity and brokenness. Psalm 61 is a song of struggle, prayer, and desire. David frequently found himself in situations where it seemed the entire known world was against him. In this particular Psalm, he is far from home. When he was younger, he was anointed to be king. He was chosen by God himself to lead the nation, yet he finds himself far from the throne, the place where he knows he should be. He is hiding out because the current king, Saul, had lost the kingdom by his own doing. Out of jealousy, King Saul is consumed in pursuing and eliminating David.

I think we all can relate to David. I'm not saying that you've been chased by a deranged king, however, I think you can understand the feeling that life is stacked against you. You know where you want to be. You have an idea of what life should look like. Yet when you look around, life is nowhere near what you thought it would be. Your mind starts filling with negativity and you start blaming yourself. Instead of moving forward, you are paralyzed by fear, anger, and/or worry as your mind is overwhelmed. In Hebrew, the word overwhelmed means to be buried beneath a huge mass of something. This is what self-loathing does. It wants to bury you underneath the weight of inaccurate thoughts that cloud your ability to imagine a future beyond where you are right then.

What is David's response? He needs a rock.

Have you seen Free Solo?

I like the Amplified Version of the Bible because of how it highlights certain words to clue us into the deeper meanings behind the scripture. Look at the passage we've been discussing:

From the end of the earth I call to You, when my heart is overwhelmed and weak; Lead me to the rock that is higher than I [a rock that is too high to reach without Your help].

Psalm 61:2 AMP

What I love about Psalm 61, specifically verse 2, is that it reminds us that we cannot navigate an *"overwhelmed and weakened"* mindset on our own. We need stable footing. We need something secure to fix our feet upon so we can move forward. David cries out for a "rock." David needs to be able to stand in the midst of being wrought with negative thoughts. In order to stand up, he recognizes he is going to need help that can only come from the Lord. David reminds us that God doesn't abandon us in these moments when our minds are flooded with negativity. He doesn't leave us to fend for ourselves. We don't have to make the climb up onto the "rock" on our own. Besides, even if we tried, we could not. We need the help of God to reach what is beyond our ability to do in our own strength. We can't "free solo" an overwhelmed mind. In other words, we need help. We can't do it on our own.

Often, as a rock climber, someone will message me this question: *"Dave, have you seen the documentary Free Solo?"*

It is perhaps the most popular rock-climbing documentary in the world (although I must say I prefer *The Dawn Wall*). Free Solo is an Oscar-winning film that has helped escalate the popularity of climbing, helping it become mainstream. I dare you to watch it, allow it to stress you out, then by the end you'll get inspired and visit your local climbing gym.

Usually, the next question I get is, *"Do you free solo (solo climb)? Is that what you do?"*

I'll give you the short answer: *No.*

Amongst the diverse types of rock climbing, it's the one that most won't touch because of how dangerous it is. "Free soloing" is rock climbing above 30 feet without gear. No ropes. No harnesses. No partner. Zero margin for error. You succeed or you fall to catastrophic consequences. It is so dangerous that less than 1% of active climbers do it. So no…I don't do it. You probably shouldn't either.

Why talk about this in regards to being mentally overwhelmed? I feel it is a picture of how so many people attempt to attack self-hate and negativity. They "free solo" it. They navigate the challenge of it alone and ill-equipped. There is something ingrained in us as humans that we *should* be self-sufficient; we feel that our vulnerability is weakness, that we have to go it alone. We end up isolating ourselves. We hang onto our collective selves by our emotional fingertips, hoping we can make it. Please, friend, hear my heart: you don't have to deal with it in this way. Isolation is what the darkness wants. Don't appease the shadows by giving it what it wants.

In Psalm 61:2, you can see it spelled out in the Amplified version. David knows he cannot deal with a mind submerged in negativity without the strength of God's help. He needs to climb up and out of his darkness, but knows that "free soloing" through personal darkness is not only dangerous, but it can also be deadly. I'm not trying to sound melodramatic. This is reality. As you'll read in this book a few times, the enemy works in isolation; God works in community. You can't do this alone. None of us can. We need help.

"You are There"

How does God help us through this? In two ways: He gives us His presence and He gives us His people. We must recognize, first, that God's presence is promised to us. In fact, a careful reading of the Scriptures will show you that the most frequent promise in the Bible is God saying, "I will be with you." Since the Garden of Eden, God's presence has never left humanity even though humanity often tries to operate separately from God.

God's omnipresence is a fact. It is truth. You can't outrun Him. You can't hide from Him. You can't sin so deep that He stops loving you. You can't hurt so much that He will avoid you. You can try to push God away, yet He will still be present to you, reaching out to you, waiting for you to open the door to your heart so he can greet you with unimaginable warmth and comfort. David said it best,

I can never escape from your Spirit!

I can never get away from your presence!

If I go up to heaven, you are there;
if I go down to the grave, you are there.

If I ride the wings of the morning,
if I dwell by the farthest oceans,
even there your hand will guide me,

and your strength will support me.

*I could ask the darkness to hide me
and the light around me to become night—
but even in darkness I cannot hide from you.*

To you the night shines as bright as day.

Darkness and light are the same to you.

Psalm 139:7-12 NLT

David was known to have seasons of joy and seasons of darkness, times of victory and times of brokenness, and moments of celebration and moments of sin. Through the highs and the lows of life, David knew that God's presence was a fact of life, not a religious theory. He knew that there was nothing that he could do to negate the fact that God's presence was always there. God never left him even when David felt he didn't deserve His loyalty.

God's presence is promised to you and to me. At the same time, we must be careful to not equate God being present with us at all times to God placing his stamp of approval on our actions and behaviors. I often hear people misappropriate the presence of God as if *"He is with me and loves me no matter what I do."* True, God will love you regardless of what you do. Nevertheless, His love is not an endorsement to do things contrary to His holiness, His character, and His commandments. Similarly, I strive to love my kids in the way our Father loves us. NOTHING could ever change or compromise that regardless of the decisions they make. That said, my love doesn't mean I approve of their decisions. My love for them does not mean that I don't confront them with my concerns about their choices. My love doesn't mean I won't discipline them. Love does all of that. Love without challenge is hollow at best. (Please do remember that discipline without love is abuse.) God loves us. His presence is with us. When we go through our darkest moments, guess what? He is close.

Even when I walk through the darkest valley, I will not be afraid, for you are close beside me.

Psalm 23:4 NLT

God's presence is not dependent upon my senses; His spirit is at work whether I can see or feel Him. God's presence is there to help me in ways I cannot help myself. He provides what I lack in my humanity. His strength helps when I have none to offer. God's presence fills the parts of me that are depleted. He guides me when I can't see the righteous path in front of me. He comforts me in moments of despair in ways I don't know how I would go on without. God offers His presence.

Secondly, God offers us His people. During my first experience rock climbing, a young man from our church was belaying me (holding the rope in a device to make sure I don't fall or become injured). On one of my first attempts up the wall, I remember slipping, plummeting downward, and the rope catching me just about a foot from the ground. My belay partner lowered me the rest of the way, then stood over me with a smile, helping me up and said, "*See, it's fun to fail!*"

He proceeded to explain to me that he was there to not only keep me safe but to help me process the climbing route I just fell from. We turned to the wall and processed the route I had taken. After some discussion, we devised a plan, and I got back on the wall and completed the climb. I got down, high-fived him, and looked for the next route to take. I've always been thankful for that seemingly small moment. It really puts things in perspective, both in the climbing gym as well as other parts of life. As an added bonus, that very same young man ended up becoming my son-in-law four years later! I love you Josh, I am so grateful you are a part of our family.

That moment really encapsulates what God's people (the Church) *should* bring to our lives. Friends, mentors, counselors, and connections are there to be present when we fall and to help us process what we were journeying through. Some of you are looking for convincing evidence of God's presence. I say, look no further than to see the presence of the people that we call "the Church." I'm talking about those people in your congregation, faults and all.

Now I get that people, both within and outside the Church, haven't always come through; there are undoubtedly times when you could have used a hand (or ear) and did not find one. Worse, there will be times when well-meaning friends make the wrong move or say the wrong thing. Unfortunately, that happens. We are all human, after all. Have you been let down by pastors? Me, too. Have church people hurt you? Me, too. (Let's be real, plenty of people outside the church have hurt me, too.) Have you discussed confidential information with trusted people only to have it get out to others? Me, too. Again, we must remember that the Church is made up of humans that are just that: human. Broken and unrefined human beings. They are a work in progress, just like the rest of us.

I don't say all of that to develop an expectation that everyone is going to let you down, rather to help you understand that *this can and does happen to all of us*. I'm not excusing the hurt that has been inflicted upon you by people. I'm trying to explain that when you live and operate in a world of imperfect people, sometimes those flawed people do things incorrectly. It doesn't stop me from leaning into people for help and community. It does challenge me, however, to be wiser with who I lean upon.

Please don't misinterpret this as saying that you should avoid leaning on people, specifically, in the Church. PLEASE, DO NOT. You cannot do this by yourself. We should not steer clear of all people. We should steward our stories. We need to make sure we know who we are leaning upon, make sure they can handle what we are giving them, and trust the intentions of their hearts.

I must admit that I have entrusted information to people that were ill-equipped to handle what was shared with them. I have mistakenly freely given details of my life to well-intended people who genuinely wanted to help, but didn't possess the abilities to process things in a healthy way, therefore they either misguided me and/or weren't able to constructively guide me. They were not the right people to lend help in my time of need (I'm sure you can relate to that experience). Their hearts may have been good but their capability to help was lacking. I've come to realize that I can't give out sensitive information about my struggles to people who don't know how to keep confidence, or those who may not have my best interest in mind. Let's be real. There are some people who "fish" for information, not because they want to help as much as because they want the power of knowing something about somebody else, something that can be used as leverage or to get a little extra attention for being in "the know." What I've come to understand is that people who "fish " for information are typically only "fishing" to feed on me, and not to help me. The relationship will quickly become parasitic. If they're doing that to me, they're doing the same to others. Take a moment to consider this: those people who gossip TO you about others will gossip ABOUT you when you are not around. Please know who you are sharing your heart with.

If you are looking to climb out of the shadowy rut, you're going to need people. *Get the right ones.* It may take a couple (or a bunch) of tries. You will find there are a lot of people who are available! You are going to learn which of your friends you should lean into as strong and stable "belaying" partners who will be with you every step of the way regardless of what your feelings tell you. You've got God's presence. You've got God's people. And now you can look in the mirror and realize this truth:

You are never alone.

Eroding Self-Hate

Now that you know you are not alone, I wanted to give you some practical steps you can take to start removing the self-hate from your life.

• Find an accountability partner to process your emotions with. This can't be just anyone who you think would volunteer. You need to find a trustworthy, Christ-centered person who will have your best interest in mind and give you level advice.

• Take an inventory of your strengths. You can do this with the help of your accountability partner if it makes the task more bearable. Be sure to write out a physical list, so you can periodically review it, and look at it whenever you feel that self-loathing rising up.

• Learn how to accept compliments. I think we instinctively know the difference between flattery (manipulation) and true encouragement (building up). When someone compliments you, instead of shrugging it off, say "*thank you*" and accept it. You deserve it.

• Cut yourself some slack. Show yourself the same amount of compassion that you would show someone else in your situation! Grace isn't just meant for you to give others, you need to give yourself grace, especially during shadowy times. Loving your neighbor as you love yourself is not just about loving your neighbor; God is saying we are to love ourselves as much as we love others!

• Take note of the differences between facts and feelings. Draw a line down a piece of paper. On one side, write out what you are feeling about the moment. On the other side, write out the facts of the situation. Learn how to recognize that feelings are important, but they make terrible masters. They clue us into what's happening, but we can not let them take the lead.

• Forgive yourself. Forgiving yourself doesn't mean you shouldn't learn from your failures and mistakes. It means you don't need to continuously add to the pain of a moment long past. If God has forgiven you, if you have a humble heart, then it's okay to forgive yourself. Take a deep breath, say a quick prayer of thanks to God for teaching us how to forgive, and move on.

Survival Tips for the Shadows:
Make a Declaration

To use a Christian culture reference, I am not a *"name it and claim it"* kind of Christian. I don't preach any type of theology that says, *"God will never tell you no."* Or, *"Whatever you pray for, God will give you."* It's a misinterpretation of Scripture and certainly hazardous to your faith.

That said, I do subscribe to making declarations.

Declarations are a part of life.

You *declare* income on your taxes.

You can *declare* bankruptcy (not the Michael Scott way).

At customs, you must *declare* what you have bought and are bringing home.

A President can *declare* a holiday.

Congress can *declare* war.

In Biblical terms, a "declaration" is a message or a word which makes the truth about something known.

From a Christ-centered perspective, when you "declare" something, you are making known or acknowledging the truth of what God has revealed to you through his Spirit or in His word. You're not creating a new truth or a new reality; you are making known what is already true. You are recognizing the truth of who God is, what God has said, and what God has done, which is your spiritual truth. This is nothing new, as it's clearly shown over and over in Scripture. To declare that God is a healer is not revealing new information, but acknowledging and bringing focus to the healing power of God. Why is it good to speak these truths aloud? I believe that when we have an outward (ie, physical) response to an inward experience, we solidify it in our lives.

Depression wants to paint inaccurate pictures of God, of ourselves, and of our relationships. When we declare what we know is true of the Lord and ourselves, we are reminding our hearts about what our feelings can mask.

In addition to acknowledging the truth, when making a declaration, you are inviting change to take place in the heart of your audience. This includes you. Again, *declaring* does not make up truths or create a new reality. It confesses what is truth and what is already reality. When that happens, you invite change in the people who hear it. How does it change a person? It invites them to bring their faith, heart, and life into alignment with truth.

When you or someone you know are navigating the shadows, *declaration* is a powerful tool. I've had friends speak into my darkness *declarations* of God's presence and help. They've *declared* God's goodness and ability over me when my emotions were telling me lies. When my friends are struggling with depression, I have had the opportunity to declare the power of God over them. From speaking scripture to proclaiming the truth about Jesus, *declaration* is a great way to remind your heart of who God is and who you are to Him.

Get a journal and start writing out some declarations about the Lord. Here are a few examples to get you started:

"I declare that God is my help and my salvation. Whom shall I fear?"

"I declare that the Lord is my strength and my song."

"I declare that I will see the goodness of the Lord in the land of the living."

"I declare that I am never alone. God is with me and will never abandon me."

Make a page of declarations in your journal or write them out so that you can use it to speak truth out in the face of the shadows that want to overwhelm you. Declare who God is, what God said, and what God has done. Speak them out loud and invite change into your heart and your mind.

- 9 -

THE COVER UP

When darkness tries to roll over my bones
When sorrow comes to steal the joy I own
When brokenness and pain is all I know
I won't be shaken, no, I won't be shaken
'Cause my fear doesn't stand a chance
When I stand in Your love
There's power that can break off every chain
There's power that can empty out a grave...

- "Stand in your love" - Bethel Music and Josh Baldwin

I look up to the mountains— does my help come from there? My help comes from the Lord, who made heaven and earth!

Psalm 121:1-2 NLT

During the state stay-at-home order of the COVID-19 pandemic of 2020, we all had to adapt to a new life that was so foreign to us. Restaurants were closed. Many houses of worship were quiet. Lots of businesses ceased operations. Schools and jobs began to work virtually. Streets were quiet. People didn't leave their homes. It was an eerie time.

Two bonuses that came from that time. A huge benefit of the pandemic was the massive amount of family time we had. I admit that I got tired of TV but it *was* fun to connect with my family over puzzles and board games. My wife and I have always taken walks together, but during this time we started walking more as a family. What a great way to reconnect with our (now young adult) children.

The second bonus was what we saw in our neighborhood. Families were outside hanging out in their yards. This reminded me of years ago prior to video games and the internet when kids actually went outside to play and get dirty. We'd walk by and say "hi." Sometimes we'd have a conversation from the other side of the street. Other times, we'd just wave at the other parents and give that look that says, "*We get it. We're all in this together.*"

Then there was my first trip to the grocery store. Everyone was masked. Nobody looked at or acknowledged each other. The streets were quiet. I remember going home and saying something to my wife about the strange ethos and remarking about how it wouldn't be long before I was going to be doing some virtual counseling. As a pastor, I knew it was only a matter of time before phone calls and messages were going to pour in. I knew that we were not meant to live this way. *God works in community.* Something was going to happen; something was going to break within us.

Unfortunately, I was correct. Emails and social media messages started coming in left and right. The isolation combined with the breaking of the "normal" flow of life created a sort of crossroads for people. They were forced to come head-to-head with issues that they could no longer run from.

One of the most common subjects in messages was about people's marriages struggling. We fielded many calls about the loneliness of people feeling cut off and isolated. The more I read and the more I listened, I began to realize something. NONE of the issues that were appearing were new to these marriages. They were surfacing from days, weeks, or months of being buried deep within. These marriage issues that seemed to be introduced to the marriage by the COVID season, were actually just revealed by it. The problem(s) had always been present. By slowing down the pace of their lives, the under-the-surface issues came to light. These couples were discovering what had already been present in the marriage. It's just that their busyness was distracting them from any awareness or recognition of the issue.

• "*COVID is causing us to fight over the kids.*" Or, has COVID made you realize that you've been living in disagreement, but you've never addressed it?

• "*The quarantine is making us fight more.*" Or, with having to see each other every day, are you now facing the fact that you need to work on conflict resolution?

• "*Being stuck at home has driven us apart.*" No, it hasn't. Perhaps it's revealed how different you've become and has shown you that you need to reconnect.

• "*We're home all the time and it's shown how different we are.*" Nope. It just shows how disconnected you had already become. It's time to do something about that.

Coming out of that incredibly difficult time for our nation and our world really caused me to look internally. Why? I began to ask myself about what was lingering beneath, not just the surface of my marriage, but the surface of my life. Was there something I've become too ignorant of because of the busyness of my "normal" life? Were there things that I thought I could outrun, outwork, or that I just hoped would just go away on their own?

Outrunning, outworking, ignoring… Let's be real, none of those options really work when it comes to what is happening internally. If anything, they might feel like they're working. After a while, something happens and reveals that none of our issues really went anywhere. Refusing to deal with things only buries them deeper. The deeper we bury a problem, the more roots it can grow into our lives.

"You are not the MythBusters"

My son and I have watched every episode of MythBusters on The Discovery Channel. If you've ever seen it, you must admit that the personalities on the show were very entertaining, and the experiments they'd do and the science behind their myth testing was absolutely fascinating.

One specific myth they worked on came from the movie Cannonball Run. It was an '80's classic where a car drove so fast it was able to "skip" across a small body of water like a rock skipping on a lake. They worked the angles. They thought through the physics behind it. To make a long story short, they successfully "skipped" a car off of the water and drove away. The trick is having a high rate of speed and a smaller body of water. If the speed was decreased, the car would have sunk. That would make for great TV, but it would be a horrible day for whoever was driving. By the way: Please don't try this at home.

This is my story. This is my song.

When it comes to depression, work and being busy serve as my cover-up. This comes naturally to me. Hard work is a staple of being a Barringer. Work ethic is a very high value to us. In my family, you're expected to be the first to volunteer. You need to be an example to others around you. You're willing to put in extra time or effort when no one else will do it. We reach out to help others before we help ourselves. We could care less who gets the credit. We'll do whatever we can so that others will shine. Again, nothing here is necessarily wrong or bad. In fact, I'm extremely thankful for this heritage that my parents passed down to me from their parents. This is what I've passed down to my kids.

Like anything good, this strong work ethic can be manipulated to be used as something unhealthy and harmful. Do I want you to have a strong work ethic? Of course. What we have to see is that there's a difference between working hard to be productive versus hiding behind my work ethic so I don't have to face reality. I became a workaholic as a way of coping with life. I was tired. I was weary. Slowing down life enough to face my depression wasn't an option. So, I lived week in and week out, covering up my darkness by staying busy.

Staying busy *seems* like a good strategy. When my schedule is packed, the darkness *seems* to be kept at bay. The more packed my schedule is, the less likely issues appear to rise. That's what busyness does. It makes you think you're dealing with the issue when all you are doing is going fast enough so that you don't have to focus on or recognize the issue. There's a fear that if you stop, you'll drown. Having a faster-paced life doesn't solve anything. It only *feels* like you are improving.

I think this could be why many people haven't noticed, or been aware of, the triggers to their depression. A solution to avoiding depression and its triggers has been to live at such a high rate of speed that you can "*skip off the surface*" of what wants to drown you. You tell yourself to "*keep going, keep moving, stay busy, and don't stop.*" Why? "*If I stop, I will go into a depression.*" We get our "fix" off our busyness as it makes us feel better that we've been productive while staving off the shadows.

Therein lies a huge issue. What you think is "helping" or "preventing" is doing neither. It's simply delaying the inevitable. Like a lion crouched in the weeds waiting to pounce, the shadows don't go away because you are too occupied with other things. Your depression is driving the incessant need to stay buried in activity while building up stronger in order to devastate you on the other side of your packed schedule.

It's time to stop playing games with depression. It's time to be honest with ourselves. It's time to drop the smoke-screen antics and be real with what we are dealing with. Depression isn't something you cover up. It's time to suit up and fight back.

Stop Wearing Makeup

The global beauty industry is worth approximately $170 billion, with $85 billion of it coming from makeup alone. This isn't a new phenomenon. Makeup has been around for centuries. As King Solomon said, *"there's nothing new under the sun"* (Ecclesiastes 1:9 NIV). The ancient Aztecs were known to use beetles to make red lipstick. Elizabethan era women would use coal tar as mascara and eyeliner (many of them went blind because of that). The ancient Egyptians were credited with being the first to use makeup. In fact, there's a belief that Cleopatra would have her ships soaked in perfume so that everyone would smell her arrival.

Billions of dollars go into the pockets of distributors and suppliers to do one thing: cover up. We'll cover up zits, wrinkles, scars, and even the color of our skin, to portray the image we desire other people to see. (Before I get any hate mail from anyone, I am not "anti-makeup." If you use it, more power to ya!) Yet, we don't stop there. We wear clothing to look slimmer. We wear hats to cover our thinning hair. We dye our hair to cover up gray. We cover our smells with perfume, deodorant, and cologne. All this to say: covering up is in our culture. We've grown up in it. We still live in it.

Covering up goes back to the beginning with Adam and Eve. When they sinned, instead of getting real with their issues, they grabbed the closest thing they could (fig leaves) to cover up. *"I can't let God see me like this. I can't let my spouse see me like this."* Thousands of years later, we are still following their example.

When my best friend was in high school, his mother tried to cut his hair. She made a huge mistake and ended up shaving a bald spot into the side of his head. In an attempt to fix it, she used her makeup to fill it in right before his basketball game. He didn't think anything of it until he came out of the game to take a rest and his teammate stared at his head, asking him why his hair was melting down the side of his head and neck.

Let's admit it, we all "cover up" in our own ways. We compensate what we feel are our deficiencies with the hopes that others won't notice. We'll make sure we secure our "cover-up" so that nobody ever finds out our inner-most truths. Like my friend, when we least expect it, we have a bit of a "meltdown" and people are left wondering what is going on because we've never been open about our struggles.

My name is Naaman

The story of Naaman isn't the most popular of biblical stories. His name and narrative isn't one that comes up often in pulpits and Sunday School lessons, yet, his story is a fascinating one. If we are going to talk about covering up, then Naaman is our guy.

In the Scripture, we find a book called 2 Kings. It's a book dedicated to telling the story of the kings that ruled in a divided kingdom. Within that book we meet a man by the name of Naaman. What we know of him is found in the first verse. On the outside, he's a great man. A valiant soldier. He's a man of authority. To everyone looking in at his life, they'd think, "*That's who I'd want to be like.*" The beginning of the passage is how any one of us would want our story to be told. Yet before we get to the second verse, we are told Naaman is a "*valiant soldier but he has leprosy.*" (2 Kings 5:1 NLT)

It *seems* everything in his life is exceeding expectations. He's got success, or so it *seems*, on every level imaginable. He's got authority and influence. He has the attention of those over him, and they trust him with everything. At home, everything is on point. He's got material possessions. He has a wife and family. Then like a bucket of water on a campfire, the end of verse one hits his story and dampens any momentum he had built up. If you want to know how depression can look to someone for whom everything in life is seemingly fantastic, look no further than Naaman.

Everything *can* be going well when depression hits. Life can be moving forward as planned. From the outside looking in, life is fine. In fact, life couldn't *look* better. Then suddenly something in us shifts and depression wants to come in with a "but" and cloud anything good happening.

- "I have a good job, but I am depressed."
- "I have success in what I produce, but I am depressed."
- "I am surrounded by friends, but I am depressed."

- "I'm married to an amazing human, but I am depressed."
- "I want to have kids someday, but I am depressed."

I'm so tired of those "but" moments. I'm weary from the rainclouds of depression moving in on moments when the sun should be shining on my life. That's what the shadows do. From an outsider's perspective, our life seems great. Nothing *looks* wrong. We hear people say, *"What do you have to be depressed about?"*, *"Your life is so great."*, or *"Other people have things worse than you."* What they don't understand is that we are just like Naaman. Beneath the exterior of what the public can see is something that is affecting us to the very core of who we are. We are fighting darkness day in and day out. One reason why other people don't know what we are dealing with is because we are so good at covering it up.

Without repeating everything I said of leprosy in the chapter, "Trauma of the Soul," I do want to highlight a few things about this malady. Naaman's first symptom of leprosy would have been a white rash. Following that he would have lost feeling where the rash was. Next, he developed sores that would lead to infection which could lead to loss of limbs (fingers, toes, etc.). Victims of leprosy can even go blind. This is a very cruel disease. The cruelty of it wasn't just in what was inflicted upon the body, but what it did to a person socially. IF it was noticeable, the person with leprosy would be forced into a leper colony away from their family and community.

Remember, Naaman had "everything" a person could want in life. Yet, he had something that he was covering up. For him to come forward, it would cost him everything important to him as there was no cure for leprosy. For him to be open about his condition meant he had to risk being driven away from the people he loved most. If you've ever wondered why people who have depression cover up, it's because there's something in our brain that says,

- *"People will never understand."*
- *"If people know, they'll judge me."*
- *"People are going to think I've been sinning, causing this to happen to me."*
- *"Nobody will want to be around me."*

I wonder if you are like Naaman. You see the potential outcome of "going public" about your struggles so you cover them up instead. I admit it's easier to see what other people are covering up instead of considering what I'm covering up. Back when I was a teenager, I had some friends who were drinking and thought that by using mouthwash, they could fool their parents into not noticing they'd been drinking (if the smell of alcohol wasn't evident, they had slurred words and the inability to walk straight). They never fooled their parents; they only fooled themselves. Let's be real, that's you and me. We think we're fooling others; we think we're fooling God himself, but in the end, we are so consumed with covering up that we never receive healing.

If we were all honest, I bet we'd conclude that we all cover up something. Addictions. Marriage problems. Anger issues. Eating disorders. Self-hatred. Pride. I mean, if you took a poll of all of the people you go to church with, if they were completely honest, you'd discover behind those who raise hands in worship, behind those suits and ties, are people who have something in their life for which they would like to see change, healing, or deliverance.

The truth is this: We can try to cover up for a long time, but the truth will begin to spill over the walls we put up. We can cover things up for only so long. After a while, your job will be affected. Marriage begins to get tested. You have a lack of desire to go to church or engage in community. Your upbeat temperament begins to wane. Whatever the outcome is, covering up is not static. It is dynamic. You and I were not created to cover up but to be real and vulnerable with God and each other. Preventing others from seeing what you are dealing with moves from being your "side hustle" to a full-time job. It's exhausting. It taxes your soul. On top of that, covering up is expensive. It takes time. It takes energy. It will cost you relationships. So, if this is you today, I want to challenge you that this is your day to make a change. Don't think of what this could mean for someone else. Think of what God could change in you.

Take Off Your Armor

If you understand leprosy, then you'd know that it doesn't aggressively spreading over the whole body, you could feasibly keep it covered for months, maybe even years. It can be easy to hide your issues from those who don't know you well. You can hide a lot of things from a lot of people, yet, the hardest people to hide your reality from are those closest to you. Do you want to know why those of us who deal with depression isolate ourselves? If people get close, they'll see the real "me." That's why we see this conversation in verses 2-3 of 2 Kings Chapter 5:

> *Now bands of raiders from Aram had gone out and had taken captive a young girl from Israel, and she served Naaman's wife. She said to her mistress, "If only my master would see the prophet who is in Samaria! He would cure him of his leprosy."*
>
> 2 Kings 5:2-3 NLT

How does his family know? How does this servant know? It's because he was home from battle and no soldier continues to wear armor when they are living in their own home. When he walks in the door, he lets go of the stuff he wears to protect himself. Those living in his home see him for who he is, leprosy and all.

He removed his armor.

Honesty is the first key to finding freedom. You've gotta remove the armor you've been using to conceal what you've been hiding. There's a lot we humans use as "armor" to keep people from seeing our struggles. For me, it was my workaholic approach to life. For you it could be an attitude, a hobby, an addiction, a job, over-committing to people, your children, social media, shopping, or anything you chose to do in an attempt to hide what you are actually dealing with.

Naaman had to come to the point where covering up was no longer an option. He had to take the first step into being honest with himself. It is exhausting to bear shame about your truths. The emotional toll from putting on your "happy mask" day after day can seem heavy enough to break you. I think Naaman was tired of "putting on a show," that he was finally ready to come clean and admit he needed to make a change.

In depression, playing pretend is just as taxing on us physically, emotionally, and spiritually as it is mentally. You're tired of putting on a façade at work, at church, and for friends. You get home from anything that involves people and you collapse on the couch, not

161

because the people were so demanding but because "covering up" your darkness simply took so much out of you. Have you ever thought about that? Some of you may think that people are draining, when in fact they may be not "draining" you as much as you may be depleting yourself by trying to be someone you are not, for people who only know the superficial "you."

It's time to get real with ourselves and admit we have a depression issue that needs help. If you are looking for a sign from God to tell you it's okay to be honest about your struggle, look no further than this paragraph. If you're ready to be honest with yourself, then you're ready for the second step towards freedom.

Opening Up to the Layers

Depression impacts you to the point where you are so desperate for help that you may no longer care about what people say. You might not be there yet, but trust me, this moment is coming. This is when you realize that suffering in isolation is more painful than coming clean with your struggles. That's why it's key to vocalize it to others.

Look at the layers happening here. We've talked about layer #1, Naaman had to be honest with himself. When he did that, layer #2 opened to where he had to be honest with his household. This can be difficult, as you wonder if talking about what you are dealing with is going to drive away or scare off the people you need most: your family. Culturally, the household included those who served the family. In this instance, a servant girl spoke up and offered hope to Naaman.

This may not seem like much in our culture, but this girl was taking a huge risk. Naaman could have rejected her counsel out of a sense of pride and arrogance. "*Who are you to tell me what to do? I can deal with this by myself.*" Isn't that what we all do, especially with the people we are most familiar with? Instead of receiving help, we snapback, often out of our insecurity, trying to protect our ego instead of allowing someone to come alongside us to lift us up and support us.

Culturally, it would have been inappropriate for a servant to speak this way to the family he/she was in service to. Naaman could have flexed his authority and had her jailed or executed for speaking to someone of his influence and power in this manner. Yet, he was open to his household. He was ready to receive help. And that led toward layer #3: inviting in an authority figure. You need someone "above" you in knowledge, expertise, and experience, to speak wisdom, direction, and accountability into you.

Verse 4 tells us that Naaman approached the king. Not only was he exposing others to his leprosy, but he was also potentially exposing the royal family to his sickness. At any point, the king could have either executed Naaman for bringing leprosy into the palace, or could have banished him to a leper colony to never see his family again. Why would he take all these risks? Naaman was at the point where hiding was no longer an option. For him to get help, he had to get past the layers that he had guarded himself against to get the help he so desperately needed. To approach the king was to humble himself, asking for accountability and support in his journey toward a healthier life.

It's not overly dramatic to say that approaching an authority figure can be a very difficult thing to wrap your head around. Getting real with someone you directly report to, a pastor, a teacher, an accountability partner, a boss, a parent, really, anyone you allow to be in any authority in your life, is laced with some inherent risk.

"What is he/she going to think?"

"How is my boss going to respond?"

"What will this cost me (in terms of advancement, promotion, or finances)?"

Then again, bringing people into the reality of your depression is always going to be risky, regardless of their relative (hierarchical) status. Not everyone will respond the way you want them to. Not everyone will say kind things, and sometimes people may be blunt or insensitive and not even realize it. Not everyone will know how to react in a positive or healthy way. Not every pastor will have the insight or understanding to help in the moment. Maybe they should read this book to equip themselves. Albeit risky, the price of honesty is still better than the toll of covering up your emotional fracture. To step forward can lead toward healing. To stay concealed can keep the infection in, staving off the joy and peace you deserve.

I love the king's response. When he hears what his officer is dealing with and what he needs to do to get help, he gives him these words,

"By all means, go…" 2 Kings 5:5 NLT

You see, Naaman was never going to find healing by staying where he was. He needed to get up and go. To continue to stay where he was wouldn't lead toward anything good. By putting himself out there, he was positioning himself for a miracle. I'm not sure who needs to hear this, but the shadows don't want you to open up. The shadows want you to continue wasting your energy hiding. Infection grows in the darkness. Just like the enemy works in isolation. The way to attack the shadows is to bring what grew in the dark (depression) and expose it to the light.

Remember, that's how the earth began. During all of the chaos of what was unformed, God spoke these words,

"Let there be light." And there was light. Genesis 1:3 ESV

When you get healthy community around you and you vocalize what you are dealing with to them, you are essentially speaking *"Let there be light"* into your shadows. You are inviting healthy people from the layers of your life into the world you live in. These layers of individuals can be a powerful tool in watching, encouraging, strengthening, and empowering you to live a joy-filled life.

The Right Help

As Naaman headed to seek the prophet of God, he took a load of merchandise to essentially buy a miracle. What I see here is this idea that many people have when it comes to their theology. *"I'm struggling. Therefore, God must be mad/displeased with me. I have to do something that will garner God's favor towards me so I can get some help."* It breaks my heart to hear people who carry this misunderstanding of God. Their depression has painted God as a tyrant and themselves as a lowly "nobody."

PSA: There's NOTHING you can do that will make God love

you more or love you less. God loves you. He is obsessed with you. What you are going through in your life is not about God's anger or disappointment in you. Do I know the reason you are dealing with depression? Nope. Do I know why I've dealt with it most of my life? Nope. What I do know is that God is for you, and me. He wants goodness for you, and me. He desires a relationship with you, and me. He was so serious about humanity that He made a way for salvation (forgiveness, hope, and eternity) for everyone, that impacts our lives today, as well as our lives someday (eternity).

Lastly, get the *right* help.

Naaman needed help. However, he didn't just need any help, he needed the *right* help. I often think people who struggle with depression will try to get some help, but it may not be the actual help he or she needs in that situation. Your pastor is great, but is he/she trained in dealing with depression? Your best friend knows you better than most, but is he/she equipped to give you an objective, healthy, Christ-centered perspective? Your parents have been around you your entire life, but can they adequately diagnose and prescribe the best treatment for getting you healthy? Sometimes when you unveil your depression to the wrong person, you set yourself up for further disappointment. You need the *right* help.

Find yourself a Christ-centered counselor. Ask for referrals. Research their credentials and background. Don't close your eyes and pick a name from the screen after you Google "local counselor." *Get the right help.*

Don't Stop Dipping

So Naaman went with his horses and chariots and stopped at the door of Elisha's house. Elisha sent a messenger to say to him, "Go, wash yourself seven times in the Jordan, and your flesh will be restored and you will be cleansed."

2 Kings 5:9-10 NLT

When Naaman went to Elisha's home, he didn't get the prophet, he got a messenger. He didn't get the Jedi, he got the Padawan. Just like we would expect, it doesn't go well. I'll admit, I'd certainly be frustrated. All of that travel and I get a messenger instead of the master. Naaman is furious. On top of that, the instructions from Elisha are simple and Naaman doesn't want to do them.

Why is Naaman so angry? It's because his expectations have not been met. Maybe he had an idea about how his therapy or healing *should* have taken place. Perhaps he wanted a bit more of a dramatic response. I mean, he brought a load of expensive cargo to present to the prophet to help earn his favor but doesn't even get facetime to present his gifts. Disappointment is what happens when there is a gap between what we expected versus what we experienced. Some of you have had that in lots of areas of life. You have this huge expectation. Then an experience follows that doesn't quite match up to what you anticipated. You end up walking away with this sensation of discontentment.

> *"Go, wash yourself seven times in the Jordan, and your flesh will be restored and you will be cleansed."*
>
> 2 Kings 5:10 NLT

To be expected to do something so simple confused Naaman to the point of anger. As you read the following verses, you can feel the rage in his heart.

> *But Naaman went away angry and said, "I thought that he would surely come out to me and stand and call on the name of the Lord his God, wave his hand over the spot and cure me of my leprosy."*
>
> Kings 5:11 NLT

He was looking for something dramatic. Instead, he received such a simple response, from someone without rank or title. You see, when you get the right help, you need to follow the path the help gave to you. Don't chase after the things you *want* to do that you *think* will make you better. You need to do the things that will actually help. I've seen this happen with people all the time. They see a counselor ONCE and think that was enough. As someone who regularly provides counsel, it takes a few meetings to establish an appropriate relationship and get the "lay of the land" before creating an action plan and beginning an effective therapeutic regimen. What is more frustrating is when the person has been given action steps that will begin to restore their health, yet they won't do them. "*I know me better than anyone.*" So my question is, why did you seek out help? Were you just looking for someone to tell you what you want to hear? If you are asking for help, *take the help.* Follow a healthy Christ-centered direction.

Thankfully, Naaman's servants speak up,

> "*My father, if the prophet had told you to do some great thing, would you not have done it? How much more, then, when he tells you, 'Wash and be cleansed'!*" *So he went down and dipped himself in the Jordan seven times, as the man of God had told him, and his flesh was restored and became clean like that of a young boy.*
>
> 2 Kings 5:13-14 NLT

You see, in their culture, when you meet up with an important person, you need to present yourself as dignified as possible, ESPECIALLY when you are asking for something. Naaman was most likely in his finest clothing, if not, in his finest armor, to display his own prominence before a prophet of God. When the prophet's direction is for him to wash in the water, it means he has to stop covering up, strip down, and expose the very condition he's been hiding to everyone. This is a humbling act. When he heads down to bathe in the Jordan River, he's not just embracing the direction he was given to walk in, but he's embracing the prescription he needed to engage in.

We all can put up fronts to people. I've done my best to cover up my depression, especially on Sundays, to the people I preach to. However, keeping the cover-up going for the sake of impressing others, or fooling people into thinking I am less flawed, does nothing good for any of us. Others are getting the fake "me." What we need to realize is that we are short-changing our community by not sharing our true selves. We are getting less out of our relationships because people are relating to the imitation "us" instead of the real, raw, vulnerable self we are trying to keep under guard. Strip off your armor and get to work on getting healthy.

I love the little details of Scripture. The number seven represents completion in Biblical literature. The idea we gather is that God wanted to heal him, not just for the day or for that month, but God wanted to give him complete, permanent healing, from the inside out. For him to receive a miracle would have bolstered his faith, strengthened him mentally, encouraged him emotionally, and obviously made him physically whole. Seven dips. Complete healing.

I think there's also something to be said of "dipping" multiple times. Not only does this signify God will bring about complete healing, but it also hints toward a responsibility that Naaman had to go down into the water seven times. I imagine him thinking after the first couple dips, *"I don't see change. I'm not feeling any different. Why should I keep doing this?"* Why do I know that? When you're navigating depression, you're attempting to do everything you know to do, maybe even what a counselor or a therapist has told you to do.

- *"I made my gratitude list and I don't feel different."*
- *"I've tried these meds and nothing seems to be changing."*
- *"I've gotten out of the house a couple times and everything still feels the same."*
- *"I followed their instructions but things still feel off inside of me."*

I get it. I've been there. When you get help for your depression, you must remind yourself over and over that despite your feelings, healthy actions ultimately bring healthy results. You cannot expect that everything is going to be set right in your life from just a couple of attempts at healthy living. It's like doing sit ups for one day thinking you will wake up with six-pack abs the day after. You can't follow instructions for two or three days and expect the 30 years of emotional darkness to be fixed. You must stay at it. Keep trying. Keep working.

Naaman, keep dipping. Healing is coming. Have faith.

Do I believe God can give immediate healing? I absolutely do. I have seen it. I've experienced it in my life. Sometimes God doesn't just drop it in our lap but has us walk things through (or, in Naaman's case, dip things through) because there's more healing within us that needs to occur. God perfects us through this process. We know from reading Scripture that Elisha could have come out and healed

Naaman. God could have used someone else to come and pray over him. I contend that leprosy wasn't Naaman's only issue. Perhaps his faith also needed healing. Maybe his skin condition took a massive toll on his mental health. Could it be that making him follow instructions and inviting Naaman to be an active part of the process created a more complete healing than an immediate healing?

Drop it Like it's Hot

To you, my friend who's reading this, I want to implore you to strip off your cover-up. Drop the façade you use to try to fool the people around you. Drop the armor you're using to protect yourself from everyone. Stop hiding behind the "front" you've used to keep people at a safe distance. Do you want healing? I know I do. Healing can't take place while you're busy hiding. Don't allow the shadows to convince you that there's no one to talk to, that there's no faith community there for you, that there's no clinician that can meet you at your place of pain and walk you toward complete healing. Is there a risk? There absolutely is. Yet, I've learned that isolation never healed anyone. It only hid me from a community that could have helped heal me.

Step into the light.

• Find family or close friends you can be honest with.

• Find a church family you can connect with.

• Find someone (a pastor, an accountability partner, and/or a clinician) to bring your life into accountability.

• Most importantly, re-find your faith in Christ.

Let Christ lead the way. Completely follow the direction He gives. If you do that, I do believe the Lord will lead you into freedom.

Survival Tips for the Shadows:
A Prayer for the Shadowy Season

Have you ever written out a prayer? Growing up in the Pentecostal Tradition (Assemblies of God), there seemed to be more of a focus on "spontaneous" prayer instead of what may be considered a more traditional/liturgical approach. What I mean by that is my church background really emphasizes what seems more "Spirit-driven" or "Spirit-led" versus traditions which include more repetition. Before my Charismatic friends write to me, I'm 100% for that style of prayer. I feel that makes up a majority of my prayer life. However, there are times I've leaned upon prayers I found in Scripture, as I'm sure many who follow the traditional prayer styles can relate to:

• *"Oh, that you would bless me and expand my territory! Please be with me in all that I do, and keep me from all trouble and pain!"*
   - Jabez (1 Chronicles 4:10 NLT)

• *"We do not know what to do, but our eyes are on you."*
   - Jehoshophat (2 Chronicles 20:12 ESV)

• *"Why must I wander around in grief, oppressed by my enemies? Send out your light and your truth; let them guide me."*
   - David (Psalm 43:2-3 NLT)

• The Lord's Prayer (Matthew 6:9-13 NLT)

There's something about leaning on the prayer of another who faced trying circumstances that brings faith to my soul and strength to my heart. There are many more than these few examples to look up and lean upon. They're great to highlight in your Bibles or to keep handy on your Bible app. Yet, there's still another challenge I'd like to give you:

Write your own.

Write out a prayer that you can keep in your journal to read when times get dark. Put ink to paper. Lay out a prayer that you can lean on that is personal; a prayer that is not from the lips of another, but directly from your heart. Place a copy in your Bible. Keep a copy in your journal.

When you feel the darkness trying to cloud in your life, wield this weapon and begin to speak faith to your storm.

- 10 -

WHERE DO WE GO FROM HERE?

Cause You're the God of the breakthrough
When I'm breaking down
You'll be working a way through
When there's no way out
This one thing I know, You're still on Your throne
So whatever I'm feeling
I've still got a reason to praise

"Reason to Praise" - Benjamin William Hastings / Caleb Culver / Cory Hunter Asbury / Ben David Fielding

"When you go through deep waters, I will be with you. When you go through rivers of difficulty, you will not drown. When you walk through the fire of oppression, you will not be burned up; the flames will not consume you."

Isaiah 43:2 NLT

I grew up an avid television junkie. Most meals were enjoyed on a TV tray watching classic sitcoms with my sister and parents. Don't worry, I was one of those kids who *actually* played outside with friends in the neighborhood. Also, as a child, I was quite the reader. My parents still talk about finding books hidden next to my bed that I would read when they thought I was asleep. My favorite series was "Little House on the Prairie" (judge me all you want, it's one of the best).

Television was a "go to" for my family. My dad particularly enjoyed watching sports, especially football. To this day, I love watching a game with him. My mom would intentionally bring tasks home from church to work on in the evening with the TV on. I remember sitting in the living room watching shows with her, even doing menial tasks to help her get her church office stuff done. We spent many nights stuffing envelopes and folding Sunday morning bulletins while watching shows together. It might not seem like much, but I really valued those moments of helping her, enjoying quality time even amidst her busy schedule.

It was during those years I really fell in love with several different series of shows; shows that I still watch reruns of even today. When I'm working on projects in the house, I will re-play some of them and find myself reminiscing on when I had seen those shows for the first time. I mean, there's something about re-watching that pilot episode that started a whole series off, and you get to go back in time and really appreciate how the characters developed. Then there's the first episode of each season that is designed to get you hooked and pique your interest. It made you wonder how the storyline was going to play out that year, kicking your imagination into gear. Back then we had to adjust our schedules so we wouldn't miss anything. These were the years before we had the ability to record anything unless you were lucky enough to have a VCR with programmable recording capacity. If you missed an episode, you had to hear about it from someone the next day.

I always dread hearing that my "favorite" TV show is ending. When you have a favorite show, you don't want it to end. Knowing it's coming to a conclusion is bad enough, but is there anything more frustrating than a favored show having a lackluster series finale? You've invested hours of time and emotions into the characters and their storylines, only to have the ending leave you to say, "*That's it? That's all they gave me!?*" Now, I recognize that not every series can have the finale of *M*A*S*H* (it set records four decades ago that are still waiting to be broken). We're not asking for that. Can't we just have an ending that leaves us satisfied, with some sense of closure?

A simple Google search will give you plenty of lists of television shows whose finales were "underwhelming" to say the least. Series like *Lost, Seinfeld, Scrubs, Rosanne, Two and a Half Men, Game of Thrones, and How I Met Your Mother* seem to be in every top ten list of the worst series finales. (I'll admit: I haven't seen most of those shows. I'm still disappointed enough by *Lost*.)

The final chapter of a book is like a series finale. It's difficult to write because you want to give that satisfying conclusion that everyone is expecting. And therein lies the difficulty completing a book like this. You are reading this chapter wondering, "*Did he beat depression? How did Dave finally rid himself of the shadows?*"

The problem is this: my struggle isn't completely over. I'm a human being who has plenty of victories in my battle with depression, but the war is far from over. Every time I think I've got the shadows beat, they rear their ugly head as if to remind me, "*I'm still here.*" What's changed in me over the years is that a disruption from depression no longer causes me to lose heart. Now, when the shadows show

173

themselves to me, I look back, square at them, and remind them, *"Yes, I'm still here, too. I'm not going anywhere. You will NOT have victory over my heart and soul."*

How have I come to that point? I wish I could put my finger on that ONE thing I did to overcome my personal darkness. I'm sure I could sell quite a few "self-help" books that list the *"3 Keys to Getting Rid of Depression Forever."* If only such keys existed!!! While I can't claim to rid you of your depression forever, what I can do is give you some of the factors that have come into play in my journey with depression that have helped guide my steps and introduce me to a healthier, happier, and more balanced life. I can say now, in my late-40's, that even though I've dealt with depression for as long as I can remember, now it hits me *less frequently* and with *less intensity* than ever before. I will NOT take that for granted. Depression is not something you can just declare defeated and gone forever. I actively engage in healthy practices knowing that it may want to come back, which it unfortunately has. Like a man who has a leaky roof, you don't wait for the rain to remind you to fix it. You work on it when the sun is shining so that when the storm rises, you are set up to be protected and dry. This final chapter is a list of what I choose (or have chosen) to engage in to get my life on a healthier pathway. These are in no particular order, so please review them all and see which speak to you.

I Talk to Jesus

I actually hesitated starting this list with prayer thinking that you (the reader) were going to roll your eyes thinking that I was going to give you a line that says, *"Just pray and everything will be better."* Do I believe in the power of prayer? ABSOLUTELY!!! That said, most people forget two basic things about prayer. First, prayer is not a parachute. Many people will turn to prayer at their last resort. *"I've tried everything. Now I guess all I can do is pray."* Prayer should be your very first response. Like calling 911 at the sight of an emergency, when there's trouble in my life, my first response is to take it to the Father. When I pray, I'm in a conversation with God. I lean into His presence and confess my pain, I ask my questions, and I silence myself to listen. Prayer cannot be a parachute. It's not your last-ditch-effort to get help. It is the perfect lifeline for all of life's events. The more you talk to the Father, the more you lean on Him, in good times and in bad, the more comfortable you will become and the more easily you will recognize His voice when he speaks to you. God longs for us to share our triumphs and failures with Him. He loves when we spend time in His presence and longs for us to share all things with Him. Don't be afraid to share even the smallest thought, whether it is gratitude or a request, with Him. Let him really know you, the comfort He can provide you in despair is unrivaled.

This leads me to my second thought that people misunderstand about prayer: Prayer is less about getting something from God and more about posturing yourself for God to work within you. We've stepped into a mode of thinking that God is a genie in a bottle; a cosmic vending machine there to give us what we ask for regardless of whether or not it is nutritional to our lives. Like spoiled children, we often throw fits when we ask for something we want, and God gives us something we need rather than what we specifically requested. Often in my prayer time, God will not give me the freedom from a struggle, instead He strengthens me with the resilience to push through the struggle. In the end, I'm a better human, husband, father, and pastor because God chose to change something in me rather than my situation.

I get Professional Help

I enjoy sitting with people and talking through their life challenges and triumphs. Notice I didn't say "*I like when people are grappling with life.*" I really love when people are willing to get help, and I feel extremely honored to be asked to be a part of that. Often when people ask me if I provide counseling, my response is the same. "*I'm willing to sit down with you and give you some pastoral wisdom. I'm honored that you'd ask that of me, and I'm proud of you for seeking out help. However, please know that I'm not a professional nor am I a replacement for a licensed counselor.*" I feel that's an important distinction to make. Unless they have specifically studied and become a licensed counselor, clergy should recognize their limitations when it comes to diagnosing and providing care to those struggling with mental and emotional health.

With all of that said, please don't be offended. I'm glad you may have a pastor or spiritual leader in your life to talk to and glean advice from. I celebrate the clergy and the church leadership you seek help from. I love that you want to get their perspective, wisdom, and direction for your situation. These people are important, and I am thankful for the pastors God has placed in my life for their support during pivotal or trying seasons.

At risk of offending some pastors reading this, unless your pastor is a licensed clinician, I would really encourage you to see a bonafide counselor. I'm not saying the minister at your church can't help you, but without the education and proper preparation for topics like depression, there can be advice and direction given that may not be healthy for you. Of course a pastor should be able to give you biblically sound advice, but they may totally miss a need for medication, further assessment, or worse, they could miss the signs that someone is going through hardship to the point where they consider harming themselves. I wouldn't be who or where I am today without the great pastors who have led and mentored me. I am also very thankful for the counselors in my life. I'm thankful for their listening ear and the abundance of wisdom they have been able to pour into me. I am grateful to know that I have been looked after on these multiple levels, and that there is now an abundance of licensed counselors to choose from to look after our mental health in our very rapidly changing electronic, post-pandemic era.

Please do me a favor and give your local clinician at least three sessions before deciding whether or not they are a good fit for you. The first session is all about laying out the groundwork for future sessions. Additional sessions are more focused on establishing a rapport with the counselor, developing trust, and then finally getting into the depth of your very individualized needs. It will take time; it will take investment. Getting help from the right person, combined with an appropriate amount of time spent both in-session and on post-session "homework", builds healthy pathways for you to work through the shadows.

I Fortify My Faith

A few years ago, we had some very heavy rains hit our area. Those who lived near the local lakes were in very real danger of their homes flooding from rising water levels. Our township provided a ton of bags and an enormous pile of sand for residents who needed to protect their homes by fortifying their yards in the face of the flood waters. This is the illustration that best describes what I've needed to do in my relationship with Christ. The flooding of darkness wants to overwhelm my soul and destroy my trust in God, so I need to build and fortify my relationship with Him to keep my faith strong.

As much as it can feel like it, depression is not the absence of God's presence. In fact, it's a place where we can truly experience a faith that is absent of any "additives and preservatives." By that I mean sometimes hype and emotions can play with our feelings and "juice up" our faith. Don't get me wrong, I'm a Charismatic Christian and thus, I'm not against emotional or passionate experiences. I enjoy being a person who loves passionate and exuberant worship services, exciting preaching, and powerful prayer times. Yet there's something about a faith that can exist, first without hype, and second, in a season of struggle where every feeling wants to push you toward hopelessness. My depression has challenged me to reinforce my faith and make sure that it's in Jesus and not in emotions, people, the church, a pastor, a denomination, or in circumstances.

Depression has caused a ton of questions about my faith in Christ. It has invited a lot of tension. Faith is supposed to have tension; it was never meant to be easy. There's tension between what your eyes see and what you know in your heart. There's tension between what you are feeling and what you intellectually understand. There's tension between what God has spoken and what has yet come to fruition. Faith invites tension. True faith is choosing to live in that tension.

Have you ever shot a bow and arrow? A bow is in constant tension between two sides. Faith is that bow. It lives in tension between what *is* what *should be*. There was a time in my younger days where any tension in my relationship with Christ was avoided at all costs. I felt that any stress on my faith would bankrupt it. I'm not sure why I felt faith was that fragile. Perhaps it was MY faith specifically that I perceived as fragile. It is of my opinion that we've raised a few generations, some of which are now leading the church, who've grown up not questioning God enough (or who were made to believe they couldn't/shouldn't ask hard questions of the Lord, the Scriptures, or the Church).

Is it of any wonder why we've seen a slew of well-known church leaders abandoning their faith and/or "deconstructing" their faith? Have we set ourselves up for disaster because we avoided tensions in our faith? Have we hurt the move of God through His Church because we didn't allow space for meaningful questions to be asked? Have we mishandled those who were bold enough to ask the questions that were on their hearts? I don't throw all of the blame at the Church, but I do think we need to shoulder some of it. We can do better with the younger generations. We must do better.

Depression will bring tension to your faith. Do not only recognize that, but welcome it. Like grabbing a dumbbell and working out, the tension that you thought would break you can be the very thing that strengthens your faith. So the question is, how do you fortify it?

Don't wait for the waters to rise before you build up your faith in Christ. Like training for a race a week before it starts (which I've done and do *not* recommend), trying to reinforce your faith when you are facing depression is extremely difficult. There's already a lot working against you, so adding tension can feel like the stress or shadows become amplified. Here's a tip: *work on* and *work out* your faith before the shadows show up. Engage with your church community consistently. Ask good questions to a mentor in your faith. Work hard to listen twice as much as you talk. Be bold enough to ask hard questions to God in prayer. Journal about them. Look to serve others to build their faith. Trust me it will build yours as well. Study your Scriptures and ask both God and some Christ-centered peers even more questions. Have coffee and have some Christ-centered discussions with people. Being proactive with your faith outside of the shadows will better prepare you to engage with God in the midst of them.

When you fortify your faith in the light, then it enables you to lean into the tension with your faith intact. Better said, you can put into practice in the darkness what you've learned in the light. Think of it like a sports team. Practice is great for preparation. Game day is proof of your preparation. Depression doesn't have to swallow up your faith. It can be transformed into an avenue to live out your faith.

I used Medication

I'm very thankful for my friend Jarrid, for whom this book was

dedicated. He was a dear friend, and the one who convinced me
to talk to my doctor about taking medication for my depression.
He didn't try to prescribe anything for me. He didn't push any
specific one on me. His goal wasn't to get me on meds. Jarrid only
encouraged me to talk openly to my physician and to get their
advice and direction. After meeting with my doctor, she started me
on some antidepressants, clearly expressing the goal of being on
them for a season, not for the rest of my life. Both my wife and I
really appreciated that. (SIDE NOTE: have your spouse or a very
close friend help walk you through this, both for accountability and
support. I even encourage letting them attend the discussion with the
doctor to help hear what you may miss as those appointments can
carry a lot of emotional stress.) My doctor also said that I needed to
be patient, as it takes 4-6 weeks to build up in my system, before we
would know if it was the right prescription for me.

It wasn't.

The first medication had side effects that I didn't enjoy. My wife
also saw behaviors in me that were undesirable. We gave it a good
season of a "try" before we sat down with our doctor to explain how
they made me feel and the reactions I was having. She gave us another
prescription as there are dozens of medications that can help with
depression. The next one worked well. I felt more level. My thoughts
seemed to be more clear. Even my staff noticed and commented on
my attitude and demeanor in the office. In fact, one of them said,
"*We like Dave on meds.*" As much as that made me smile at knowing
that the meds were working, I felt frustrated at myself for not
getting on them earlier, but I was also frustrated for not being able
to "conquer" depression without medication. The medication would
have helped me sooner if I had gotten over my pride and used these
available resources.

After a few years and a few life changes, I began to sense a physical
shift in my body. I hear this happens as you get older. My physical
health was fantastic. I was running. I started rock climbing. I was
eating better. The pace of life I was living was more balanced. As such,
I expressed to my wife that I wanted to know her feelings about going
off my medication. Of course, I didn't need her permission to make
a medical change. I don't need her permission for anything (nor does
she need mine), however, I *did* need her unity and support.

We believe what the heart of *Psalm 133 NLT* conveys. This scripture tells us that where there is unity, God will command his blessing. For that reason, we approach each other humbly, willing to hear the other person. This leads to my second reason for asking her input: I don't have to live with me, she does. My wife is my accountability in life, as well as my partner. I wanted her insight, advice, and partnership in this. I felt like she should be as much a part of this decision as I was.

Together, we went to the doctor and talked through the components of the decision. I wasn't taken off my meds immediately, rather, slowly and carefully. Doses were lessened; Anne was very vigilant in observing. We knew that if this didn't work, I would go back on an effective dose, and I was okay with that. Me having peace of mind and soul was worth taking meds if that is what was needed. There was no shame in needing medicine, especially when we saw how much they helped me to become balanced after such a long time of dealing with the shadows. For me, now in my 40's, something shifted, and after a while, the medication was no longer needed. Will I be forever off them? I have no idea. What I do know, is if the darkness returns to a level that I am unable to control independently, I'm willing to own the situation, and take the necessary steps to be healthier, and not to waste so much precious time struggling if there is a better pathway to becoming balanced.

I Write Things Down

Journaling was something I would have not envisioned getting into. Writing in a journal felt like I was a teenager with a diary. "*Dear diary, Dave feels terrible today.*" I've seen enough cheesy TV shows with people writing in them that journaling seemed sappy. It was something I simply wasn't interested in. There were friends of mine who journaled and would go on and on about what it did for them. They'd talk about how many pages they would write and, personally, I didn't feel like I had that capacity, nor did I have the interest.

It was during a season of depression that I found myself immersed in "my Psalm" (*Psalm 42*). That day, something changed in me. It's as if God gave me a view of the Psalms, not simply as songs and poetry, but as if they were journal entries. I felt reading the Psalms was helping me peer into the heart of some very human (ie, emotional) leaders dealing with deep thoughts, both good and bad.

Maybe it was the seemingly raw, unprocessed approach of the Psalmists that I connected deeply with. Some of the chapters seem written with an unfiltered heart; with no concern over who would read their words. Yet these words were not "venting," rather they were the bleeding of the heart to express the richness of emotions they were experiencing. The more I read, the more I began to see the writers developing perspective through their own writing. Over and over in the Psalms, you can feel the chaos of what the writers were experiencing and how the love and mercy of God overpowered what the darkness was trying to establish.

The Psalms gave me "permission;" a sense of freedom, to journal in a raw way to articulate just needed to express. Just as the 150 chapters hold so much variety in length, subject, and style, I felt the Lord release my pen to transcribe not a form, but a moment. I didn't have to step into a style, but I could work out what was in my heart. Some days, my journal pages have looked like Psalm 117 (the shortest Psalm). Other days are a bit more like Psalm 119 (the longest Psalm). Length didn't matter; the moment of journaling, the ability to process and release an emotion, was the goal.

In a world of reactions, we need more careful thoughts.

My advice to you is this: First, buy a journal. Something that suits you and is comfortable to hold (let's be real, if you don't like the look of it, you're not going to use it). Second, start simple. Date the entry, write down a few thoughts, maybe reflect on your day. No one is going to read this. No teacher is going to grade this. Write a few sentences. Write a whole page. This is your space to process whatever you need to think through. Third, designate a journaling time. Do *not* attempt to schedule this time when you are normally falling asleep. The point isn't about the moment of the day but to create the opportunity to work out thoughts and emotions. Lastly, make it accessible. I keep a journal in my backpack. You may have it in your nightstand. You may have more than one if that simplifies its accessibility. If you don't have the journal nearby, you'll likely forget it even exists. Make sure it's around so that you'll have it as a tool to navigate the shadows.

I'm a Part of a Christ-Centered Community

I know what some of you are thinking, "*Dave, you're a pastor. You have to go to church.*" True. What I need you to see is the difference between "*going to a church*" and being a "*part of a church.*" It's kind of ironic that I'm writing about this on a day I ran into an acquaintance who asked me how our church was going. He then said, "*We've got a great church, but I'm not plugged in yet. We're still new to the church.*" When I asked him when they started attending, he told me it had been four years.

Four years. Four years of attending yet, not feeling like they were a part of anything. My challenge to him was to get connected and to find a way to be a part of what God was doing in his faith community. It's easier to distance yourself (especially during times of depression) if you are not intentionally involved. Being withdrawn sets you up to miss access to the amazing resources that being a part of a church family provides.

Will your church "family" have issues? Absolutely. Is anyone perfect? Well, if any of them claim they are, they're lying (that includes the pastor). You need the church, and the church needs you. That's why the Scriptures used the metaphor of the "body." Regardless of who you are, you are a part of what God wants to do in your community. What part are you? Well, that's for you to discover as you get involved. Will your role or your participation look like that of others? Most likely, not, which is the beauty of being just one part of the whole.

What has being a part of a church done for me? It's given me a support system of friends, leaders, and mentors that have walked me through my darkest times. It was at worship services where I found people who would listen to me, pray with me, and check in on me. I would have meals with people and create lifelong connections. The more consistent I was with attending and being involved with the church, the more opportunities came for meeting new people and deepening my relationship with others, which, in turn, developed a deeper relationship with God.

The church also became an outlet for me to serve. One of the most therapeutic things you can do for your mental health is to do something with the sole intention of blessing others. There's something about looking to give that causes this boomerang effect where you end up discovering blessings in your life just because you decided to offer help or encouragement. The Scripture says, "*...those who refresh others will themselves be refreshed.*" (Proverbs 11:25 NLT). The choice to serve is intended to bless others. What the Scripture points out (by God's own design) is that when we look to bless others, we end up being as blessed as those we were serving.

I repeat myself: There's no such thing as a perfect church nor a perfect pastor. People are human. People are imperfect. Have you been hurt by a church and/or its leadership? Me, too. Has it made you think about disconnecting from the local church? Me, too. Yet these challenges helped me determine where I would attend and what I was willing to be a part of. Please remember to show others wisdom and grace as you find a church. Help create a healthy congregation, following the example Jesus has laid out for us.

I Got My Body Healthier

In the winter of 2005, I dropped a trailer on my leg. That resulted in a trip to the Emergency Department. During that hospital visit, I had some alarming test results in terms of my physical well-being. My heart rate, cholesterol, weight, my actual leg, and everything in between, was a mess. I remember telling the Lord it was time for a change as I was laying on that hospital bed. What I didn't expect was the change that came next.

After two years of watching my eating habits, I dropped 77 pounds! That was something to celebrate. After a few more years of good eating habits and running regularly, I dropped another 50 pounds. I not only felt better physically, but I began to feel better mentally and emotionally. As stated in a previous chapter, the body is tightly connected to the soul and the spirit. When one is affected, good or bad, the other parts are also impacted. Over time, my bouts of depression began to become less severe and occurred less often. What I had intended to do to help myself physically ended up having positive mental effects.

Hear my heart: this isn't about becoming a specific shape or size. Getting healthier wasn't specifically about my weight, but my mortality. In the hospital, I told myself, "*I'm turning 30 and I want to have a long life with my family. I cannot keep this lifestyle."* I didn't realize at that point that being healthier wasn't just about the longevity of my life, but it was also about the quality of the life I would live.

Do something positive for your body. Start today. As far as exercise, try subscribing to a podcast and listen to it on daily walks (shameless plug: check out my podcast called "Marriage Monday"). Run with a friend. If you think you can't run, do "Couch to 5K" (this is what my wife used to get healthier) or even the old-school classic, "Sit and be Fit". Go biking. Join a gym with a friend. Get on a treadmill and watch a TV show while you walk or run. As far as food, cut the junk out of your diet. Stop drinking pop (or what non-Michiganders call "soda"). Eat proper portions. Don't eat after a specific time of evening. Dive into fruits and vegetables. As far as the pace of life, get proper sleep. Watch overcommitting yourself. Schedule downtime and welcome boredom. Take a nap here and there. Go to an art gallery or museum. Make "fun" a mandatory part of your life.

As you become more healthy on a physical level, don't be surprised to see how much healthier you become emotionally, mentally, and spiritually. It's all connected. Tending to your needs in one area should have positive effects on the others.

I Found a Close Circle

Regardless of whether you are an introvert or an extrovert, the one thing that is certain is that we all need people. I'm not saying you need a lot of people, or you need to constantly be with a group of people. However, you need to have consistent human contact with others, especially if you deal with the shadows.

Two of the hardest parts of depression is this feeling like you don't want to be around anyone and/or the feeling that no one would want to be around you. You may give off an ethos to those around you that says, *"stay clear of me today."* I've done that plenty of times to my wife, my kids, and my staff. It's a self-preservation mode. I feel overwhelmed and want to distance myself from people, so others don't add to the burdens I'm already feeling the weight of.

Depression by itself already makes you feel alone, even though that may not actually be true. When you start pushing people away, it positions your feelings to mix with reality, creating a very dangerous situation. *"I feel alone. I've pushed so many people away…Now I am actually alone."* Isolation isn't a bad place to visit, but it's a horrible place to live. Sure it's nice to have some alone time, but dwelling in a bad mental space, alone, will only make it worse. Remember, *the enemy works in isolation.*

I've had to work hard to establish solid friendships that I can turn to when I face my darkest moments and times of doubt. I'll admit, these are not the easiest to find or cultivate. To clarify, it's not hard to find people who want a place of influence in others' lives. I think I can easily make a lineup of people who want to have some sort of "say so" in my life. What I need are not those who volunteer but those whom I can *deeply* trust. Those who have my best intention at heart, who have a strong relationship with Jesus, who have time to devote to our friendship, and, whose confidence I can trust in, to keep my private information private. These relationships can take time to develop, and you may find you have different friends which play different roles.

I've got friends for ministry questions.

I've got friends to argue sports.

I've got friends to hang out with and have fun.

I've got friends to be creative with and bounce ideas off of.

If you position yourself to meet new people at work, church, or in your neighborhood, for example, you will find groups of people to connect with for these various reasons. It takes intention and effort to differentiate between those who are willing to be present at your darkest moments and those whose support and wisdom you can trust when you feel like you can't think straight. They may not be the same. Some people want to be present but may not be equipped to help you in a healthy way. You need the right kind of individuals who you can lean onto without concern of over or under-reaction. You need people who are not quick to judge, but can be rapid responders in prayer, encouragement, and unconditional love.

When I came forward and began to openly discuss my struggle with depression, there were a ton of people who reached out to me on social media and volunteered their help. I'm grateful for their willingness to be available for that. It felt nice to have so many reach out. What I needed, though, was people who were dedicated to giving up the time and energy it takes to become trusted friends. I needed people who understood my situation of being a pastor and the pressures it brings. I needed people who see confidentiality and integrity as the highest of priorities. I have friends, and had friends then. For the shadows, though, I need the support network to be the right friends to count on at the darkest times. I needed a close circle of friends.

Perhaps my favorite series of all time is the miniseries called *Band of Brothers*. The dramatized account of a team of paratroopers follows them from basic training all the way to the end of WWII. These men learned together, fought together, bled together, and looked out for each other. I know this sounds intense, and maybe a bit dramatic, but these are the types of friends I need for my depression.

I need people ready to rally to my side when I'm hurting the most.

I need people ready to pray and fight the battles I can't fight for myself.

I need people to watch my back and check in on me.

I need people with a tough hide.

I need people that can see through my attitude and know the real me.

I need people who know how to be present (this is more important to me than knowing the "right" things to say).

It's people like this who have helped me through my "*darkest valley.*" (Psalm 23:4 NLT). They are my close circle. They are the ones who've gotten me through the roughest times.

I Built Momentum an Ounce at a Time

During my weight loss journey, I had found myself very discouraged. I remember thinking I was not just plateauing, but I felt as though I was on the verge of falling backwards and gaining all the weight back. I began to avoid my accountability partner at work. He would normally check in with me once weekly to see what my weigh-in was. I remember avoiding him throughout the normal "check-in day." He popped into my office to confront me. *"I know why you've been steering clear of me. Tell me what your weigh-in was."* To understand my frustration, I was used to telling him that I was down two, three, or four pounds that week. I seemed to have a lot of immediate success, making it easy to face him every week, but that particular week, I didn't want to tell him what the scale told me.

"I only lost one ounce."

I'll never forget the look on his face. He was absolutely dumbfounded. I thought he was going to give me a bit of a talking to about the lack of headway I made that week. What he was confused by was that I avoided him, not because I gained weight, but because I didn't have the measure of success I thought I should have. Then he said something very profound that I will never forget.

"Whether it's a pound or an ounce, progress is progress, regardless of its amount or size."

That lesson has never left me. I've spoken this over marriages, singles, addicts, and, yes, even those with mental illnesses. Our culture customarily celebrates huge leaps forward. We commemorate big accomplishments and feats. So much so that I think we've lost the art of celebrating every bit of progress. When you're dealing with inner darkness, sometimes an ounce of progress is all you can find. Even a single ounce means you are moving in the right direction! Forward progress builds momentum, regardless of its amount or size.

Do not despise these small beginnings, for the Lord rejoices to see the work begin...

Zechariah 4:10 NLT

Refuse to look down on small steps forward! What I think a "win" from this book would be, is for you to begin to move forward in the healing process (or, if you are reading this on behalf of a loved one who deals with depression, a win would be to make a step forward in helping others find hope and healing). Sometimes you'll take huge steps and it will actually feel like you're making strides. Other times, you'll see only mere ounce-sized movements forward. Please don't despise small beginnings. Remember, the Lord rejoices in seeing the work begin. If the Lord can rejoice in your small beginnings, in the movement of an ounce in the right direction, certainly, you should be able to rejoice in the small steps, too!

Progress is "momentum." Any step ahead, regardless of how big you (or others, for that matter) think it is, is another mark of momentum and a day of victory to be celebrated.

So, this brings us to a final question: Where do you go from here? Well, it depends upon your reason for reading this book.

For the "Support Staff":

If you are reading this book and have never had to deal personally with depression, first, thank you for investing your time to develop an understanding about something you may have previously been in the "dark" about. Since my initial blog about depression in 2014, I am frequently asked to help others understand what depression is, what it feels like, and how to approach the people in their lives who are dealing with it. If that is you, I consider you to be "Support Staff" to those people in your life navigating depression. I would implore you to do a few things for those in your life who face shadows of their own.

• **Be fully present.** Put your phone on silent and set it aside. Get rid of distractions and listen to your friend with both of your ears and both of your eyes. Engage them in conversation. Asking questions is okay. Listening is even better. Be quick to listen and slow to speak. You don't have to say all the right things, you just need to be present for them.

• **Watch and pray.** Be willing to fight spiritually for your friends and intercede over their lives. Pray with your friend. Pray over him/her when they're not around. Every prayer of yours matters. Be vigilant of their behaviors and be sure to be more involved when you notice they are withdrawing.

• **Follow up with them**. Many times, people will ask us how they can help. Few actually follow up or check in to see how we are doing as time goes on. Set yourself apart as that friend who refuses to allow someone to hurt alone.

• **Volunteer yourself to help your friend get help**. From helping your friend find an appropriate counselor, to driving them to appointments (even make yourself to go in with them, *if they'd like you to*), show your friend you will be there with them every step of the way. Offer to make them a meal or take them out for ice cream (ice cream makes everything better). Do they want silence? Ask if you can silently sit next to them and watch a movie together. Being willing to invest your time and energy in them will make a huge difference. You may need to be a little more outgoing than normal, but as long as they are receptive continue to offer what you have to give them. Knowing someone is not scared away by their moodiness may have a bigger impact than you could imagine!

Remember, you don't have to always know what to say. Your time and your attention will go a long way and can matter even more than word choice. Feeling they are loved can provide a healthy dose of encouragement to a depressed soul.

Now, for the Other Audience...

If you are reading this book because you deal with depression, I have a few challenges for you. First, find a next step. Go back into this chapter and note some things that you may not have attempted to lessen the darkness caused by your shadows. Don't pick three or four to try all at once. That's an easy way to become overwhelmed. Stick to one task to begin with, two at the most, and see how applying new and consistent strategies to dealing with your depression can begin to make a difference in instilling hope for your future. Once you've gotten a new strategy integrated into your lifestyle, then come back to the book and choose another approach, and so on and so forth. Push yourself, but not so much that you are fatigued or overly anxious. Ask a friend to walk the pathway with you if it is too overwhelming to try alone.

Some examples of next steps:

Fortify your faith. What's a step you can take this week to start working that out? Sit and talk with your pastor. Buy a book on a spiritual topic that you are interested in and read a chapter a week. Carve out some time for prayer and reflection. Ask a friend to pray with you.

Get some professional help? Instead of booking an appointment with just anyone, a next step can simply be researching local Christ-centered counselors in your area. Look into who you should see. The next step can be making an appointment. Remember: It's about steps forward regardless of the size of the step. It is okay to break up tasks into smaller pieces when you don't feel you have the required energy or endurance.

Set up an appointment with your physician. Call your doctor and get it on the calendar. You can start with getting a simple physical (which you should do annually), and then discuss with them their insight into your mental health.

Please hear me out: I don't want you to worry about outcomes as much as I want you to take next steps. Each step is progress. And every piece of progress builds momentum even if it's only ounce-sized. I've listed here only a few of the strategies discussed within this chapter, to provide some examples of how to take a next step, and break it down into further steps. This is to emphasize, again (I am hoping to make a point on this one!), that a step forward is PROGRESS, regardless of its size. Progress builds momentum. You have to start somewhere.

Next, I would like to challenge you to find an accountability partner. Regardless of which step you choose to work on, get someone to help hold you accountable to your decision to move forward. It can be as simple as, "*This week, I'm going to make an appointment with my doctor.*" This allows your trusted friend to follow up to see if that happened, and if it did not, it positions them in a way to know how they can better help support you. Accountability isn't about somebody controlling you but someone holding you to your word and encouraging you through each step. As the old African proverb says, "*If you want to go fast, go alone. If you want to go far, go together.*" I want you to go far. I don't want you to get lost in the darkness. Make the healthiest choice; choose to go through this with someone along your side.

This is a pivoting point. This is your time for change. Though this chapter is done, and this book is complete, my hope is that you find yourself ready to turn the page to begin a new chapter in your life. This is a new day. This is a new time. I'm excited about what God has in store for you.

Remember: Regardless of what the darkness has spoken to you, because of Christ, you will always have hope. In Jesus, the best has yet to come for you. Live from that vision and watch your life step out of the shadows and into His marvelous light.

Printed in the United States
by Baker & Taylor Publisher Services